An OPUS book

Roman Catholicism in England
from the Elizabethan Settlement to the Second
Vatican Council

Edward Norman

Roman Catholicism in England

from the Elizabethan Settlement to the Second
Vatican Council

Oxford   New York

OXFORD UNIVERSITY PRESS

1985

Oxford University Press, Walton Street, Oxford OX2 6DP

London New York Toronto
Delhi Bombay Calcutta Madras Karachi
Kuala Lumpur Singapore Hong Kong Tokyo
Nairobi Dar es Salaam Cape Town
Melbourne Auckland
and associated companies in
Beirut Berlin Ibadan Mexico City Nicosia

Oxford is a trade mark of Oxford University Press

British Library Cataloguing in Publication Data
Norman, E.R.
Roman Catholicism in England from the
Elizabethan settlement to the Second
Vatican Council.—(OPUS)
1. Catholic Church—England—History
—Modern period, 1500-
I. Title II. Series
282'.42 BX1492
ISBN 0-19-219181-0

Library of Congress Cataloging in Publication Data
Norman, Edward R.
Roman Catholicism in England from the
Elizabethan settlement to the Second
Vatican Council. (OPUS)
Bibliography: p.
Includes index.
1. Catholics—England—History.
2. Catholic Church—England—History.
3. England—Church history.
I. Title. II. Series.
BX1491.N67 1985 282'.42 84-16563
ISBN 0-19-219181-0

Printed in Great Britain by
Billing & Sons Ltd.,
Worcester and London

In honour of
SAINT HENRY WALPOLE
Domus Sancti Petri Alumnus

Contents

Preface

The essay which follows begins at a point half-way through the English Reformation, and it ends half-way through the twentieth century. In the first location, the dust was just beginning to settle on the earlier series of religious changes; in the second an upheaval, not fully perceived by English participants at the Second Vatican Council, was impending. The history of the religious minority between these points forms the subject of the essay. It attempts to show a number of essential continuities discernible through several distinct phases: some of those phases were imposed externally through the hostile action of the State, some arose from the conflicts of interpretation that are germane to all worthwhile human enterprises, some came in response to the guidance of Roman authority. All appear to have, in a wide perspective, that unity which the local history of a universal institution ought to disclose to the observer.

E.R.N.

August 1983

1 A rejected minority

The history of Christianity is full of small religious communities and churches, existing at the margin of society, often attracting the hostility of their neighbours, and sometimes subject to active persecution. Their internal development tends to be uneven, and the very adverse conditions in which they are set seems to warp and remould their structures until they either release their members once more into the mainstreams from which they originally became excluded or simply dissolve away altogether. In this isolation they have typically produced some extraordinary excesses; many have allied themselves to moral or political radicalism. There has been a persistent religious phenomenon, much noted in the sociology of religion, in which excluded groups evolve highly sectarian character-istics. The English Reformation of the sixteenth century left the Catholics in such an excluded condition, cut off from the vital Protestant culture in which the modern State in this country was born and developed. What is most unusual about their subsequent history is that it did not follow the patterns so familiar for those in their condition. The English Catholic 'recusants'—those who refused to conform to the laws of the unitary Protestant establish-ment—did not develop sectarian qualities, did not become political radicals (though a few sought revolution as a means of procuring a Catholic dynastic restoration), did not deviate from orthodoxy, and did not, above all, quietly slide back into a comfortable acquiescence with the new order. Theirs is a noble history of enormous self-sacrifice for higher purposes, and of a rooted determination to preserve both their English virtue and their religious allegiance in a sensible and clear balance.

As with all historical change, of course, the ideals which individual Catholics held underwent considerable reinterpretation. It is not always easy to see that the Church and the faith as understood by the Elizabethan Catholic martyrs, for example, was exactly the same as the Church and the faith which presented themselves to the minds of the nineteenth-century ultramontane leaders or to the liberal intelligence of the mid-twentieth-century Church. There was, perhaps, a greater continuity, even so, among Catholics than among Protestants. The common experience of suffering for the preservation of the faith, the more exacting tests, and greater consequent clarity, which they experience who hold to allegiances *contra mundum*, gave English Catholicism a long memory and some permanent standards by which to evaluate necessary readjustments to changing conditions in the world. The most important of these standards was the sense of belonging to a universal body, the obligation of loyalty to Rome as the centre of unity. From some perspectives the history of English Catholicism is easily abridged into appearing to be a history of internal conflicts —of men falling out over how to adjust their condition to realities. But those are probably largely false perspectives, for they arrange the entire evolution of an institution around the recorded, and untypical, events of noteworthy controversy, and leave the perpetual Catholic life, as led quietly by men and women in the parishes—without controversy and without doubt—with no memorial. The great conflicts, too, were not without a constructive importance. Though sometimes, as is the way with human enterprises, personal considerations intruded to embitter some differences of view about ecclesiastical policy, and though men seem for ever given to representing their personal impulses as ideological necessities, the fact is that very important issues were at stake—the preservation of the faith itself, as in the earthen vessels of worldly judgement—and men would have been less than human had they not, from time to time, disagreed over the best course to achieve that end.

Despite the insistence on Roman authority, it is a notable feature of English Catholic history that it has remained very English. Catholics have, even in the days of severest persecution, as in the reign of Elizabeth I, always insisted on their devotion as Englishmen to the Constitution of the country and to the political values of English liberty. Among some of the continental exiles there grew up alien notions of autocracy, as practised by the foreign Catholic sovereigns who were their hosts and protectors. But in England itself there has been an enduring Catholic tradition of declared loyalism —even to the State which sought to destroy them. Sometimes, no doubt, this was a matter of calculated expediency, a way of surviving without loss of principle. That, however, proved to be controversial, and many of the internal disputes of Catholicism, through three centuries, resulted from differences of opinion about the extent of the concessions that could be made in the difficult balance between loyalty to Rome and allegiance to the Crown. The nineteenth-century ultramontanes believed that the acquiescence of English Catholics in a sort of English Catholic polity amounted to a version of 'Gallicanism'. These tensions, largely unavoidable given the hostile conditions in which the Church existed, form essential themes in any historical account of Catholic development. But let it be stressed again that they are not a summary of the usual or the local. For half of its life since the Reformation, the Catholic Church in England was dominated by the country gentry and had, for its centres, the country houses and the small hamlets. Removed by the action of the penal code from public life, Catholic survival was in the hands of adherents who had to adapt the structure of the Church to local conditions. What is remarkable is that it remained not only recognizably Catholic, but Catholic in a reasonably pure form. No heresies emerged, no revolts against Roman authority occurred. The worst result of the long disruption was the enforced irregularity of lay control of ecclesiastical property and lay appoint-ment of priests—but Rome, recognizing the difficulties, was prepared to accept these practices as necessary exceptions to general rules.

In deference to the susceptibilities of their Protestant neighbours, Catholics cultivated habits of discreet worship and careful with-drawal from occasions of offence. Newman, while preaching before the First Provincial Synod of Westminster, in 1852, spoke of the conventional impression of Catholic life in his day as typified by 'an old-fashioned house of gloomy appearance, closed in with high walls, with an iron gate, and yews, and the report attaching to it that "Roman Catholics" lived there; but who they were, or what they did, or what was meant by calling them Roman Catholics, no one could tell—though it had an unpleasant sound'. The social withdrawal of Catholics, indeed, had the reverse effect from that intended: it attracted the Protestant charge of deliberate secrecy, and encouraged popular suspicions that dark and superstitious practices took place. It was these sorts of suspicions, in fact, which formed the basic content of the anti-Catholic tradition in England—a tradition which showed a remarkable stability and persistence, and has only declined within the last century. In fact its origins lay far beyond the Reformation, in the anticlericalism and English religious particularism of the Middle Ages. At the Reformation the anticlerical impulses were divided: some continued to be attached to the new Protestant clergy, but some were deliberately applied to provide a permanently hostile critique of the Roman Church. 'Our official history', Hilaire Belloc once observed, 'has taught by continual suggestions and by taking it as if it were for granted that the English people were in some fashion naturally antagonistic to Catholicism.'

There has been a consistent production of anti-Catholic literature since the Reformation. Some of the works have been classics of English popular culture, like John Foxe's *Book of Martyrs* ('*Acts and Monuments of these latter and perillous dayes*'), first published in 1563. It went through five editions in the reign of Elizabeth I, and, with numerous subsequent republications, became the main source for most people of what Catholicism was like. Foxe represented it as inherently corrupt, authoritarian, foreign, and, above all, as implacably opposed to personal liberty. The association of English constitutional freedom, liberal institutions, and the rule of common law with national Protestantism has always involved, in contrast, a condemnation of 'popery' as the embodiment of 'medieval' subservience. State prayers of thanksgiving for national deliverance from Catholicism over the Gunpowder Plot were not removed from the Anglican Book of Common Prayer until 1859. The nineteenth century, which saw the start of widespread literacy and the development of a large popular press, also witnessed the appearance of a particularly virulent anti-Catholic literature. Some of it, like the *Awful Disclosures of Maria Monk*, published in 1836, were of North American origin, indicating the successful emigration of the English 'No Popery' popular culture. Intellectual opinion became preoccupied with vilification of papal temporal government in Italy, and made Garibaldi into a surrogate Protestant. Difficulties over the Irish question encouraged public men in the thesis that there was a link between Protestantism and economic success, for Irish peasant *mores* and Catholicism appeared indistinguishable. At nearly all stages in the development of the anti-Catholic tradition Catholicism was made to seem politically subversive, because of the 'dual allegiance' owed both to the papacy and to the British monarchy. It was assumed to be inherently superstitious: the supposed worship of saints, the idolatry thought to be involved in Marian devotions, and the 'blasphemy' of the sacrifice of the Mass. It was held that Catholic authorities used force and fraud to procure the perpetuation of their system: the first typified by the 'imprisonment' of young women in convents, the second by the cult of ecclesiastical miracles encouraged by the Counter-Reformation Church. The practice of confession was alleged to involve indecency and to allow the clergy to acquire improper influence, especially over women. At the time of the national uproar caused by the restoration of the Catholic hierarchy in 1850, one pamphleteer suggested the death penalty for any minister of the Church of England who should venture to emulate his Catholic counterparts by hearing confessions. These notions formed part of a multi-class culture. Anti-Catholicism was just as strong, and depended upon the same sort of evidences, for both the Protestant intelligentsia and the unlettered masses. Occasionally a few faintly perceived that the actual Catholic clergy of England were unlike the historical model devised by Protestantism; they conceded that priests could be blameless and even dedicated, if deluded. The author, William Tayler, of *Popery: Its Character and Its Crimes* noticed this in 1847, but had an explanation to hand. 'We do not ask what Romish priests are when surrounded by Protestantism', he declared, 'but what, where the system develops itself without restraint.' It is scarcely necessary to look much beyond such sentiments to account for English popular suspicions of foreigners, and especially of south Europeans.

Any survey of English Catholic history should always project this popular culture of antipathy as the essential background to an understanding of the remarkable survival of the Church. Instead of encouraging extremism and distorted vision, it seems to have fostered discreet heroism and a quiet determination to witness to universal principles. Some of the heroism was, through force of circumstance, not discreet at all: the public executions of Catholics, in a series of purges throughout the century and a half following the Reformation, added a martyrology to spur Catholic resistance to integration with Protestantism. In the broadest perspective it is the consistency of English Catholicism through the last four centuries which most impresses; and that despite the obvious differences of interpretation of the faith which have from time to time occurred. Catholic history has a unity. Its major themes can be traced and analysed, and its leading figures seen to have been conscious of a single purpose.

2 The Elizabethan settlement

Recent historical scholarship, in surveying the nature of English Roman Catholicism in the two centuries following the Reformation, has tended to emphasize the discontinuities. Most of the laity and clergy seem to have conformed to the Elizabethan settlement, and the new mission priests who arrived in the country after 1574 appear slowly to have accommodated to the idea of a different sort of Catholic presence in England—to an acceptance, however reluctantly, that the roots of the medieval past had been torn up and that some quite novel institutional agencies were required to replace them. One historian has even written of the Elizabethan era as having witnessed the 'death of a Church'. In this understanding of things the small communities of Catholics still scattered across the landscape after the cataclysmic upheavals were without firm guidance from the religious past: the incoherence, variety, and relative independence of the medieval English Church had left few clear indications of how to separate the essentials from the inessentials of the preceding religious tradition. Rome, in the crucial years, gave little guidance to the faithful remnant, and direction, when it came with the returning mission priests, was sharply divided between those (principally secular clergy) who continued, still, to assume the existence of a medieval order waiting to be restored, and those (mostly Jesuits) who envisaged a new Catholic life released from the old institutions. Yet continuity in some sense there must have been. The men and women who suffered enormous privations for their faith may clearly have had many kinds of reasons for retaining it, and considerable differences of view as to its actual nature: but their desire to keep the Mass, their dislike of the undisguised Erastianism of the new Protestant order, or their sense that they belonged to a universal society, was inherited from the past and was retained with a longing for a lost world which must, of its nature, have imposed some continuities. When, more than a century after the Elizabethan settlement, Catholics looked to the restored Stuart monarchy of Charles II and James II to return a legal existence of the faith, it was still the Church of the past to which they looked for their model—however imperfect their understanding of it by then was.

The Elizabethan settlement occurred at a time of considerable volatility in religious affairs. The almost universal belief in religious uniformity and in the coextensive realms of the sacred and the secular meant that the principle of *cuius regio, eius religio* necessarily operated to produce an exclusivity for the State religion, but at the same time there was an underlying sense of impermanence. Men had lived through so many religious changes since the original breach with Rome made by Henry VIII that they were unsure how the wheel of fortune might turn. The Elizabethan penal laws against the Catholics were not in themselves remarkable or unusual—and were, indeed, more or less what those who found themselves outside the official religion must have expected. It is often forgotten, by Catholic historians, that the penal code operated against Protestant Nonconformists too. Five Anabaptists were executed in Elizabeth's reign; Puritan divines were hounded out of the State Church. The nonconforming Protestants, like the Catholics, had overseas links which tainted their religious professions with the suspicion of political disloyalty or unreliability; yet it was the Catholics, through a number of episodes in Elizabeth's reign, who became particularly associated with treason, and whose connections with foreign military enterprises especially singled them out for proscription. The Catholics, that is to say, shared the general acceptance of the unitary doctrines of the State, and for long could only envisage the old faith restored through political action at the centre, so that monarch and subjects would be of the same religion. The Elizabethan penal code—whose legacy was to be of such enormous importance in determining subsequent Catholic self-consciousness in England—was the direct result of these views of the State. Both the extent of religious volatility and the immediate background of Catholic espousal of unitary notions of the State were revealed during the reign of Queen Mary.

In November 1554 Cardinal Reginald Pole presided over the formal reconciliation of England to the Holy See. The ease with which this was accomplished showed both the conservative nature of the religious changes effected by the Henrician Reformation and the extent to which the advanced Protestantism of Edward VI's reign was premature. But the restoration of Catholicism under Mary did not indicate any significant shift in the religious bases of society: it was a simple result of the religion of the sovereign being regarded as the appropriate standard for national polity. As if in recognition of this, the Royal Supremacy over the Church, the centre of the Henrician changes, was not repealed along with the other ecclesiastical legislation since the break with Rome in 1529. The clergy generally accepted the return to Catholicism—though some one-and-a-half thousand were ejected from their livings for having got married. Most of the influential laity also returned to the fold. Twelve of the bishops of Henry VIII remained in their sees or were restored to them: Cranmer, Latimer, Ridley, and Hooper were executed. In all, 273 Protestants were burned during the reign, providing the ideology of anti-Catholicism which, enshrined in Foxe's *Book of Martyrs*, was to dog English Catholicism for centuries. But by contemporary European standards—and judged in the light of steps taken by twentieth-century totalitarian governments to secure political uniformity—the executions under Mary were not especially ferocious. In the last years of Henry VIII's reign one Catholic bishop and 41 priests had been executed; in Elizabeth's reign 123 Catholic priests were put to death. It was expected that the religious uniformity of the State would be secured by such means. Nor were the burnings an indication that the restored Catholicism was particularly authoritarian, or Roman-orientated, or influenced by the Council of Trent (which had begun its sessions in 1545 and had completed its main work by the end of Mary's reign). Pole himself was a saintly man who had, it is true, lived abroad for twenty years before he returned as Legate (and as Cranmer's successor at Canterbury) and was therefore somewhat out of touch with the development of opinion in England. Yet he had been a humanist at the University of Padua in the 1530s and had, at that time, embraced reformist theology; though more conservative by 1554, his programme for the Catholic restoration in England was far from untouched by enlightened ideas. At the national synod he summoned in 1555 plans were set down for a translation of the Scriptures and for the instruction of the clergy in the duty of preaching. There were to be new seminaries attached to cathedrals in an attempt to cultivate a more educated clergy, and the monastic refoundations, of which there were seven, were clearly on reformed lines. Monastic lands conveyed to lay owners at the time of the dissolutions were, by special guarantee of the papacy, retained by their purchasers—another indication of the sensitivity of the restored Church to the reality of change in England. For all that, Catholicism did not achieve popularity: perhaps no version of ecclesiastical institutions was ever popular in England. The Queen's Spanish marriage was disliked, and was obviously linked in the public mind to the triumphalist Catholicism of the Spanish Crown. But there is no evidence, either, for any popular attachment to the cause of the Protestants, who were now either lying low, conforming, or living in exile overseas. Probably most men were awaiting the development of things, prepared to assent to the sovereign's religion all the time that it did not grossly interfere with their customary religious observances or their social standing.

The great bulk of the clergy appear to have acquiesced as readily in the Elizabethan settlement of 1559—in the Acts of Supremacy and Uniformity—as they had done in the Marian Catholic restoration. There persisted, still, the prevalent sense that the religious situation was unstable. The break with Rome was not actually formal: it was represented in the Crown's practical resumption of control of ecclesiastical offices, and the means by which religious teaching was declared, rather than in any overt and articulated renunciation of membership of the universal Church. Royal Supremacy 'in all spiritual or ecclesiastical things as well as temporal' was reactivated. A modification of the 1552 Prayer Book became the legal and obligatory service. The papacy clearly hoped that despite the changes England might yet remain inside the Church, even with so large a measure of local autonomy. In 1560 and 1561 papal nuncios were dispatched to Elizabeth's court. They were not received, and Philip II of Spain was also attempting to obstruct papal access to England. This flexible response by Pius IV was in the face of a massive rejection of the Elizabethan settlement by the Marian episcopate. All the bishops refused to take the new Oath of Supremacy and were deprived of their sees—all, that is, except for Bishop Kitchin of Llandaff, whom the Spanish ambassador described as 'a greedy old man of little learning'. The academic divines were divided. Ten heads of colleges in Oxford and Cambridge refused the oath and were deprived. Yet the parochial clergy, in general, either co-operated or quietly gave a public consent to the changes while continuing a clandestine use of the old services for those who requested them. Perhaps as many as three hundred priests were removed from their benefices: it was not a large demonstration of attachment to the Catholic rites (which the great majority of the clergy were describing now, in the prescribed homilies, as 'superstitious' and 'blasphemous'). Among the laity there was a greater preparedness to accept the new order of things or to blend it discreetly with adhesion to the old; in the north a more conservative society, existing at the extremities of centralized control, retained more obvious loyalties to Catholicism. Everywhere Englishmen disclosed a characteristically pragmatic and quasi-Pelagian preference for a kind of religious ethicism rather than for doctrinal or liturgical exactitude. 'They gave no education at all as to any religion to their children,' the Benedictine Augustine Baker wrote, 'but regarded only in them a good moral external carriage.' The Government hoped that Catholicism would fade from memory as new generations were reared in the new religious services. The atmosphere of the Church of England was still sufficiently traditionalist, with its preserved order of bishops, and its Prayer Book offices with their resonances of the old uses, to furnish a sense of continuity. The acquiescence of most of the clergy was evidence of that. Elizabeth's own religious sensibilities seem also to have retained some Catholic elements. She disapproved of clerical marriage and disliked the radical reformers—showing fury on a visit to Cambridge when some progressive students mocked Catholic liturgical practices. Known Catholics were retained at court, and even the music of the Chapel Royal was directed by a Catholic, William Byrd. Until 1570 there was no organized opposition to the changes, and hence the impression that everything might simply settle down without further disruption. With each year the old faith lost adherents as people found the compulsory attendance at parish churches (established by the 1559 legislation) a better alternative to financial penalties and social marginalization. The Marian priests were dying out, and Catholic patrons were beginning to find it difficult, either through actual shortages or through prudence, to place sympathetic priests in their livings. As it turned out, as well, the sheer length of Elizabeth's reign was helpful to her chances of success. Whatever destabilizing consequences may have resulted from uncertainties as to the succession were amply balanced by the discontinuities of papal policy—she lived through no fewer than ten pontificates.

The situation was changed, however, by the presence of external events and the growth of a positive anti-Catholic national sentiment. The sequence began with the arrival in England of the exiled Catholic Queen Mary of Scotland in 1568. In 1569 the Rebellion of the Northern Earls involved yearnings for a Catholic restoration— Mass was said by the rebels in Durham Cathedral for the first time in a decade—even though religious considerations were perhaps not decisive among the discontents that precipitated the rising. In 1570 St Pius V excommunicated the Queen, in the bull *Regnans in Excelsis*. Thereafter Catholic assaults upon Protestantism overseas, and plots to achieve a Catholic succession in England, combined to enhance a growing popular association between the old faith and political catastrophe: the Massacre of St Bartholomew's Day in 1572 and the Ridolfi Plot of the same year, the 'Spanish Fury' in Antwerp in 1576, the Babington Plot in 1586, and the Armada in 1588. By the end of the century it was possible for the Jesuit Robert Southwell to declare, in a report to Rome, that every mischief which excited the public was blamed on the Catholics.

At almost every stage in this sequence an accumulating series of penal laws was enacted in order to contain what was perceived as the Catholic threat. The Act of Uniformity, in 1559, had initiated the process: it stipulated fines and then imprisonment for clergy who declined to use the new Prayer Book, and obliged everyone to attend church on Sundays (with a 12 pence fine for those who refused). In 1563 the provisions of the Act of Supremacy were extended by imposing the oath upon lower grades of officials and by exacting the penalties of praemunire. But it was in the wake of *Regnans in Excelsis* that the first really severe legislation was passed. The bull was itself the sign that a formal break with Rome had occurred. St Pius V, unaware early in 1570 of the failure of the Rebellion of the Northern Earls in 1569 and anxious to assist the consciences of those Catholics who had risen against their sovereign, deprived Elizabeth of her title and pronounced her a heretic: 'moreover the nobles, subjects and people of the said kingdom and anyone else who has taken an oath to her are freed from that and from every obligation to allegiance, fealty and obedience.' At the time of the Jesuit mission to England, ten years later, the papacy made it clear that the terms of the bull were not binding on Catholics in existing circumstances—it was by then held to be a sort of statement of intent pending a Catholic restoration. But the effect of the bull upon the English Government was not surprisingly to stimulate anti-Catholic sentiment—to stimulate, however, and not to create: it was clear that the hostility of William Cecil and Francis Walsingham among the Elizabethan ministers was anyway sufficient to provide for an increase of legal inhibitions against Catholics. John Felton, a Catholic who placed a copy of the bull on the gate of the Bishop of London's palace, was executed for treason. New laws in 1571 made it treason to call the Queen a heretic; the introduction of papal bulls was made illegal along with Catholic devotional articles; those unable to conform with the new religion were forbidden to leave the country or to be trained overseas for ordination. These measures were passed by the first House of Commons to be composed entirely of non-Catholics: it was the first in which members had to subscribe the Oath of Supremacy. Parliament in Elizabeth's reign was always more anxious than the Queen's ministers to impose severe penal legislation on Catholics.

The legislation which followed the arrival of the first Jesuits in 1580 was intended to draw a distinction between religious and political elements in Catholicism: it was made a treasonable offence to convert people to the Catholic faith if the intention was to absolve them from their allegiance to the Crown. The harbouring of priests was made illegal, and the fine for failure to attend the services of the parish church was raised to £20. An important change was the transfer of jurisdiction in recusancy cases from the ecclesiastical to the civil courts. In some cases, the distinction between political and religious motivation in attempted Catholic ministrations operated to allow local officials to turn a blind eye to quiet or friendly Catholics, but in many others the distinction never really meant very much, and the Act became a charter for priest-hunting. From this date began the construction of 'priest holes' and other hiding places for the clergy in Catholic houses; priests were lodged in attics and it was not until the middle decades of the next century that it became normal for them to live in more public accommodation. An Act of 1585 made the mere presence of priests in England treason. It was directed against the mission priests who, according to the words of the preamble, intended to foster 'sedition, rebellion, and open hostility'. The death penalty was extended to those harbouring priests ordained overseas. Catholic parents were forbidden to send their children to seminaries in foreign countries, and students abroad had to return to England and subscribe to the Act of Supremacy. The movement of Catholics around the country was restricted by the Five Mile Act of 1593. In order to break hereditary religious allegiance, furthermore, some Catholic children of noble and gentry families were removed to become wards of the Crown and brought up as Protestants.

Had the Elizabethan penal code been rigorously enforced the practice of Catholicism in England could not, perhaps, have survived. In reality, the laws were only intermittently activated, and even then there was great local and regional variation in the extent to which officers of the Crown were prepared or were able to take action against Catholic gentry. The distinction between Catholics and non-Catholics was still in many cases unclear. Enormous numbers of people who retained Catholic inclinations conformed to the law by attendance on Sundays at parish churches in order to avoid the fine; there is evidence that some Catholic priests, too, felt able to say the new Protestant services in church and to continue celebrating Mass in private houses. These 'Church papists' were in general able to remain within the law. The recusants—those who publicly opted for nonconformity—were always a very small minority, and had mostly made their position clear from the beginning of Elizabeth's religious settlement. They were led by substantial members of the nobility, like Lord Vaux and Lord Stourton, and by gentleman landowners like Sir John Petre and Sir Thomas Tresham, and the effects of recusancy fines, accumulating over the years, were to reduce the wealth of many of them very considerably. The lesser gentry also suffered greatly. But below their social level the effects of the fines cannot have been so dire: humbler people avoided them by attendance at church or because they were not wealthy enough for the law to bother with them. Some charges of recusancy were brought for personal reasons—it was a time for settling old scores. In the 1580s the enforcement of the legislation was transferred from Justices of the Peace to special commissioners, and as these were sometimes men of noted and enthusiastic Protestantism the laws were then applied with vigour. Some landowners, like Tresham, conveyed their property to trustees in an attempt to avoid forfeiture. This sort of loophole was partially closed by an Act of 1587 which regularized the collection of fines. There was already a degree of calculation in recusancy exactions, and an awareness of their value to the Crown as a source of income: officers were anxious not to kill off the source of future revenue and this provided an incentive to levy fines moderately. The Oath of Supremacy, similarly, was not required in all cases where it might have been, although there seem to have been examples of Catholics being quite prepared to take it provided they could continue undisturbed in their religious profession. Even those imprisoned— laymen for harbouring priests, and priests for saying Mass—were often treated civilly. Elizabethan prisons were rather open institutions (the Tower of London excepted, hence its more sinister reputation), and Catholic prisoners soon converted many of them into Mass-centres, with local people coming in on Sundays to hear both Mass and sermon. The Government, in consequence, periodically cleared the priests out and banished them from the realm. Wisbech Castle, in Cambridgeshire, which the Government used as an internment camp for clergy after 1580, became a centre of Catholic learning. But the severe nature of the penal laws was at times devastating. Sir Thomas Tresham, for example, who was originally imprisoned for harbouring St Edmund Campion, spent fifteen years in gaol. And many died for their faith.

There has been, in recent historical writing, something of a reaction against the martyrology of Elizabethan Catholicism, yet it is difficult to see how else the distinctive qualities of being identified as a Catholic could have survived had not individual lives been sacrificed publicly for a clear vision of what it meant. The gentry and their dependants who continued as Catholics were largely untouched by Catholic literature, and their worship, before long, lacked the liturgical ornamentation which characterized its contemporaneous European expressions: their sense of belonging to a distinct and universal religious society was in some large measure sustained through the example of martyrdom. In 1579 St Cuthbert Mayne, a Douai priest, was executed at Launceston. The 122 other priests who followed him to the scaffold in the reign of Elizabeth were articulate witnesses to a lucid sense of spiritual exclusivity—to the Catholic ideal of a Church not subject for its essential teaching to the secular power. About half the mission priests who arrived were arrested, and about half of these were hanged, often (after 1580) suffering torture first. The noble example of their sacrifice, over succeeding decades and then centuries, became the English Catholics' most sacred centre of communal self-consciousness, a light which sustained many in the darkness of social disadvantage and civil deprivation.

The mission priests who returned to England after 1574 did not arrive in a land entirely bereft of Catholic clergy—though some, and especially the Jesuits, often gave that impression. Apart from the 'Church papists' among the clergy, there were some secular priests who had gone underground and who provided continuity with the immediate Catholic past. By the end of Elizabeth's reign around 800 priests had returned to England; some 450 of the seculars were trained at Douai. This great college, which left a strong and enduring impression upon the nature of English Catholicism, was founded in 1568 by Cardinal Allen. William Allen, who was born in Lancashire in 1532, had originally conformed with the Protestant Church under Edward VI, while at Oxford, and was elected a fellow of Oriel College in 1550. In 1556 he became the principal of St Mary's Hall, which was attached to the College, and in 1561 disclosed his return to Catholic allegiance by refusing the Oath of Supremacy. He departed to Louvain, returned briefly to England in the following year, and then, in 1565, went once more to the Low Countries and was ordained at Malines. Two years later, while in Rome, he decided to join the staff of the new university founded at Douai by Philip II; and it was there that he used the income derived from his chair to finance a college to prepare English exiles for the priesthood. In 1581, in recognition of the importance of his work for English Catholicism, he was given the title of 'Prefect of the Mission' by the papacy. He was made a cardinal in 1587, and died in 1594. Most Catholic scholars have regarded him as the saviour of English Catholicism, and as the inspiration of activism. Unmoved by those who saw little but futility in sending young priests to their death in England, Allen declared that Catholic renewal was attained by working and not by waiting. His college at Douai was not originally intended as a missionary institution, however. Allen had no early vision of a mission church. Douai was founded to provide a surrogate Oxford: a place of conventional clerical education for those excluded from their natural resort in less disordered times. The curriculum was very traditional, and the vocation of priesthood it assumed looked back to the settled territorial ministry of the past and not to a missionary situation of the future. It grew out of the requirements of the hundred or more Oxford exiles who gathered at Louvain and other European centres of learning during the early years of Elizabeth's reign. They had no radical plans for a restored Church in England, and intended to pursue their scholarship and perpetuate their priesthood until the times changed in their favour and they could return safely to their work in England. The exiles did not constitute an obscurantist fringe; there were fifteen heads of Oxford and Cambridge colleges among them, and the Regius Professors of Divinity from both universities. Just after the foundation of Douai in 1568 a second wave of academic exiles arrived—men who had some personal acquaintance with the operations and personnel of the Elizabethan State Church and were even less accommodating in their attitudes than the earlier exiles. Campion and Parsons, the Jesuit pioneers, were among this second group. It was the militants who helped to turn Douai into a more missionary-orientated institution, just as it was the Jesuits who converted the college at Rome to similar purposes after 1586. Although Allen did not have the original vision of a mission Church, however, he allowed the transformation of his college to train the seculars for a missionary role, and it was he who was instrumental in handing the control of the Roman college to the Jesuits. By the mid-1570s there were some 240 students at Douai. The monument to the intellectual life of the college was the Douai translation of the New Testament, which was published in 1582 (at Rheims where the college was temporarily resident to avoid the war in the Low Countries), and of the Old Testament whose publication was completed in 1610. The exiles in general were productive: some two hundred works of English Catholic scholarship and polemicism were published on European presses before the end of Elizabeth's reign.

The English hospice in Rome was converted into a college in 1576, and in 1577 the arrival of the first contingent of students (who came from Douai) firmly established it. The formal foundation, with papal authorization, came in 1579, by which time there were some thirty students. The English College, the *Venerabile*, was to become one of the most formative influences in subsequent English Catholicism, providing generations of Church leaders with a close acquaintance with Roman education and religious discipline. The first years of the college were marked by considerable internal upheaval—Owen Lewis, the canon law scholar who was its head, contending for a traditionalist academic institution, and the bulk of the students, with Jesuit support, seeking to repeat in Rome the success they had achieved in transforming Douai into a missionary seminary. By 1579 it was clear that Lewis had lost, and the college was thereafter controlled by the Jesuits, into whose hands it passed formally in 1586. Two years later it was directed by Parsons, who headed it until his death in 1610 and who introduced the 'missionary oath' for students: an undertaking to work in England after ordination. The Roman College, like Douai· and the English colleges at Valladolid, Seville, and Madrid, was not Tridentine—these colleges were not part of a diocesan structure and were easily adapted to a missionary function. Both because of their purpose in replenishing the English Catholic Church with potential political subversives, and because all the English colleges apart from the Roman one were in Spanish territory, the Government of Queen Elizabeth monitored their affairs closely. Servants operated as spies, and the departures of newly ordained priests for England were reported. Penal legislation, and especially the Act of 1581, attempted to isolate the mission from the surviving Catholic clergy of English training and background. Many of the Catholics on the Continent, for their part, did hope for political change in England and worked actively for it—though the priests on the mission in England, both seculars and regulars, consciously avoided political activity. Allen and Parsons met for the first time, in Rome, in 1579. Both shared a growing conviction that only an invasion of England by a Catholic power, with papal blessing, could procure a Catholic restoration. In 1576 Gregory XIII had discussed proposals for such an invasion (to be led by Thomas Stukeley) with Allen. In 1579 Nicholas Sander actually arrived in Ireland with Spanish troops but was defeated. Both Allen and Parsons seem to have supposed that the arrival of Catholic forces would initiate a spontaneous religious uprising; both failed to perceive that although the Elizabethan settlement was fragile it was also national. The Armada in 1588 completed the process of identifying Catholicism with England's enemies and with it there ended any realistic chance of religious change through force— through foreign armies achieving popular acceptance. Allen's

Admonition to the Nobility and People of England, intended for distribution after the Spanish invasion in 1588, showed no signs of recognizing that Elizabethan values had solidified around national self-consciousness. Protestantism was strengthened in consequence. Parsons's espousal of the claims of the Infanta Isabella to the English throne was similarly detached from evolving Elizabethan realities. Catholic opponents of the idea of foreign intervention, like Owen Lewis and Lord Paget, sensed not only its probable impracticability but also its variance from the buoyant values of England under Elizabeth.

It was the Jesuit mission priests who were most hated by the English Government, although their numbers in England were not large. The Generals of the Society did not regard England as a particularly fruitful prospect, and gave work there a low priority: most of the Englishmen who entered the Society on the Continent were sent to other places than their homeland. By the end of the century there were fewer than twenty Jesuits in England (and four of those were in prison). It was Cardinal Allen who persuaded the Society to take up the notion of an English presence, and in 1580 Parsons and Campion were sent. They landed in the atmosphere of heightened national distrust of Catholicism following the collapse of the Spanish invasion of Ireland. In their instructions was a clear statement that their duty was to reconcile to the faith those who had lapsed but to avoid mixing themselves 'in the affairs of state', and they were forbidden to speak against the Queen or to allow others to do so. The Government was not likely to take much notice of that, however, and a watch was kept at the ports in the hope of intercepting the two Jesuits. Their departure from Rome had been in circumstances of the utmost publicity: most of the English in the city had accompanied them to the Flaminian Gate—the place from which, a little over three hundred years later, Cardinal Wiseman was to announce the restoration of the English Catholic hierarchy. In Bologna, *en route*, Campion wrote: 'Though we should fall at the first onset, yet our army is full of fresh recruits, but by whose victory our ghosts will be pacified.' They landed separately at Dover in June and both made their way to London, and subsequently departed to different areas of the country ministering from house to house among the Catholic noblemen and gentry. In a statement drawn up for the attention of the Privy Council should he be arrested—and known as his 'Brag'—Campion repeated that his ministry had no political purpose. Parsons set up a press to produce Catholic works, first in London and then at Stonor. But the work of both Jesuits was short-lived. Campion was arrested at Lyford Grange in July 1581 and was executed at Tyburn in December. Parsons left England in October in order to report to Allen on the state of religion in England.

The importance of these two men in re-establishing a Catholic presence in England was, in different ways, enormous, despite the limited amount they could accomplish on the short mission of 1580–1. St Edmund Campion was born in London in 1540, the son of a bookseller, and was educated at Christ's Hospital and the newly founded St John's College in Oxford. He took his degree in 1564 and became a fellow of his college. At this time he was a conforming member of the State Church—and was, indeed, under the influence of Bishop Cheyney of Gloucester, ordained to the deacon's orders of the Church of England in 1569. His conversion to Catholicism, like Newman's in the nineteenth century, followed a study of the early Fathers. He arrived at Douai in 1571 to prepare for the priesthood. As a penance, he journeyed to Rome on foot, when he went off to join the Society of Jesus. Then followed six years in Prague, as a member of the Austrian Province of the Society, and it was there, in 1578, that he was raised to the priesthood. In the next year he was called by Allen to Rome with the intention of preparing him for the English mission. Campion emphasized the essential continuity of the faith. At his trial in November 1581 he declared: 'In condemning us, you condemn all your own ancestors—all the ancient priests, bishops and kings—all that was once the glory of England, the island of saints, and the most devoted child of the See of Peter.' He asked: 'For what have we taught, however you may qualify it with the odious name of treason, that they did not uniformly teach?' Campion's death must have inspired many in their Catholic profession. One is known: a young law student of Gray's Inn, who had studied at Peterhouse in Cambridge. St Henry Walpole's clothes were sprinkled with blood as Campion's body was dismembered at Tyburn, and he dedicated himself to take up the martyr's work. In 1582 he crossed to Rheims and later joined the Jesuits in Rome. He was ordained in 1588 and returned to immediate arrest and a martyr's death himself, at York, in April 1595.

Robert Parsons also emphasized the spiritual nature of the Church, the religious impropriety of subjecting the institutions which came from revelation to the political realm. He criticized the Catholic Church of the past for its lack of evangelical fervour—for not being spiritual enough, for too much involvement and compromise with the worldly powers. He was, in that sense, a disciple of the reforming spirit of the sixteenth century: he sought, like Campion, a return to the primitive purity of the Church of the Fathers, and he disapproved of the clergy under Mary for not 'renewing the spirit'. It was Parsons who most emphasized the missionary nature of the Church which was to be revitalized in England, and it was he who took over the direction of the English mission after Allen's death. He had been born in Somerset in 1546, the son of a blacksmith. In 1564 he went to St Mary's Hall, Oxford, and then went on to Balliol, where he became a fellow in 1568. He conformed to the Elizabethan settlement, and twice took the Oath of Supremacy: he was bursar and dean of his college. In 1574, on a journey to Padua to study medicine, he stopped at Louvain and became a Catholic. At Rome, in 1575, he entered the Society of Jesus, and was ordained in 1578. After his meeting with Allen in 1579 the two became close friends and collaborators—Allen's support for the Jesuits was crucial to their success. Parsons was if anything more conscious of the need for political action to overturn the Protestant establishment in England than Allen, and with the years he became increasingly convinced of this. As rector of the English College in Rome until his death in 1610, he exercised a huge influence both upon the ideals of the English mission and upon the thought of the Curia regarding English questions. After the Jesuit martyr Robert Southwell, he was perhaps the best-known English Catholic writer of the times. Parsons laid the foundations for the expansion of the English Jesuits early in the seventeenth century. In 1623 an English Province was formally constituted, and by the 1640s there were around 180 Jesuits serving in England. Their educational enterprises on the Continent, where more than half the members of the English Province continued to work, reached their most successful point with the establishment of the boys' school at St Omer in 1624.

The other regulars, also, began a modest recovery on the Continent during Elizabeth's reign, although it was, as with the Jesuits, not until the first half of the seventeenth century that numbers and institutions significantly expanded. In the forty years following Elizabeth's death, some five thousand English men and women entered religious orders, mostly in the Low Countries. The Benedictines, in the same period, founded St Gregory's monastery at Douai and St Laurence's at Dieulouard; a Benedictine convent established at Brussels in 1598 founded daughter houses in Cambrai and Dunkirk. The Franciscans established St Bonaventure's at Douai in 1629 and set up a formal English Province in the same year. The Bridgettine nuns of Sion, founded in 1420, eventually settled in Lisbon. Some of the regulars of those times were men and women of outstanding spirituality and mystical experience, like Benet Canfield, the Capuchin friar, and Augustine Baker, the Benedictine. Most enduring of these, perhaps, in her influence, was Mary Ward, founder of the Institute of the Blessed Virgin Mary and author of an autobiography which disclosed mystical experiences. She came from Yorkshire to the Netherlands in 1605 seeking a vocation, and, failing to find satisfaction in the existing orders, founded the Institute in 1610 on the Jesuit model—austere and disciplined yet unenclosed, and flexible in terms of application in the world. The Institute undertook work among the poor and set up a number of schools for girls. Houses of the order spread through Europe, and attracted the same hostility as attached to the Jesuits. By the second decade of the seventeenth century there were over sixty nuns, six of whom were in the London house. There were schools at York and in Hammersmith. Despite the suppression of the Institute by the papacy in 1631, following internal dissensions and continued external jealousies, it later revived and Mary Ward herself returned to England.

In response, therefore, to the Elizabethan religious settlement and its protective legislation, it can be seen that the Catholics re-established some sort of presence in England. What had actually happened? Had enough of the old Church survived, through the remaining secular clergy, to allow a real continuity, or did the mission priests in effect found a new Church in England? The question is enveloped in historical controversy and there can be no unqualified answer; but the probability is that much more survived the extinction of the ancient hierarchy (with the death of its last representative, Bishop Goldwell of St Asaph, in 1585) than might appear. It is certainly true that the leading Catholic clergy during Elizabeth's reign were converts, that their vision of Catholicism was often rather different from the Catholicism of the past, and that their reasons for espousing what they thought of as the Catholic faith were various and not always in accordance either with preceding English notions of the faith or contemporary Roman ones. It is also true that later Catholic apologists, especially in the nineteenth century, were to make the supposedly unchanging character of the Church the centre of their claims to authenticity based upon the permanence of creed and practice. During the Elizabethan period the nature and (by force of circumstance) the practice of Catholicism indeed changed considerably. The new activists, like Parsons, had no real links with the old Church and had been inspired by a reaction to the spiritual inadequacies of the State Church settlement: they tended to attach a Catholic label to their resulting ideas whether or not they truly derived from previous English Catholic experience. The old Church in England, furthermore, had often lacked coherence, and that made the construction of a simulation a very inexact process. With its own liturgical rite—the Sarum use—and its lay subjection to quasi-erastian political control, the English Catholic Church of the Middle Ages had anyway been sufficiently separated from Roman example or direction to offer no reliable external model. It is almost impossible to restore an institution which, in its most effective periods of operation, did not quite correspond to anything like itself elsewhere. It is, additionally, unhelpful to notice that the English Catholic Church in the reign of Elizabeth was unlike the institution envisaged by the decrees of the Council of Trent, whose sessions ended in 1563. The centralizing genius of the Council was anyway foreign to the ethos of traditional English Catholicism, and would unquestionably have run into difficulties and produced local variations in England, had there been no Reformation at all. In terms of the religious ideas of the Elizabethan Catholic leaders, similarly, there was a variance from the past: many were soaked in the Christian humanist culture and self-consciously sought a purified Church, one which made a greater individual demand upon its members. In his *Memorial for the Reformation of England* (1596) Parsons envisaged a Catholic Church, identified with the nation, that was to be characterized by zealous activism and freedom from past institutional impediments.

But all these evidences of apparent discontinuity with preceding Catholicism in England are not to be considered conclusive of a radical or intended break. There has never, in the history of the Church, been a time when Christians had an agreed agenda about their faith, and the unavoidable relationship between religious ideas and human culture, expressed through learning or through institutions, has always meant that the general outlook of believers in one period or locality has differed from that in others. If it may be concluded that the Catholics of the nineteenth century believed rather different things about the nature of their Church from the Catholics of Elizabeth's reign, for example, it can certainly be concluded that precisely the same may be said of Anglicans—or of any body of ideas and people. Elizabethan Catholics certainly, therefore, saw their Church rather differently from their immediate predecessors. The question is whether there was anything so radical in this difference as to amount to a real discontinuity.

Most of the secular clergy, both those who remained in England and sat out the changes and those who constituted the first arrivals from Douai, believed they represented a continuity with the past. For over a century subsequently, they were to press for a return of regular canonical government on the explicit grounds that they were the successors of the ancient Church. Among the regulars, too, these feelings were well represented, and in Sigebert Buckley, a Westminster Abbey monk imprisoned at Wisbech Castle, the Benedictines found a pre-1559 survivor through whom they were able to trace and to establish claims to continuity with their ancient rights. The seculars, in particular, retained a strong sense of the public and territorial role of the clergy, and awaited conditions favourable for its restoration. What little is known of the ecclesiastical ideas of the gentry suggests that they, too, had no sense that the Church which re-emerged under Elizabeth was radically different from the past, except in its enforced secrecy. It is not, in fact, accurate to distinguish too closely between the older secular clergy and the new mission priests. Overt difficulties between them over jurisdiction did, it is true, point to deeper disagreements about the nature of the Church; but these were a continuation of the sort of differences which had characterized the Catholicism of the English Middle Ages, and it was only the fact that the most dynamic of the mission orders was a recent one, the Jesuits, which introduced a really new element. The Jesuits soon came to regard the English Church as a mission, and therefore as requiring the abandonment of some of the old structures. Hence the upheavals which their influence procured at Douai, at the Roman College, and among the prisoners at Wisbech. Such differences about the nature of the Church existed in many other areas where the Jesuits were active—in the Spanish colonial empire, for example, there were very comparable disputes. The English differences of view were not in themselves any indication, therefore, that England suffered any particular peculiarities of discontinuity or that the Jesuits were responding in a unique way. Their view that the mission in England was to a more or less permanent minority, to a sect in society and not to a nascent Church, corresponded to reality, and by the 1620s they were especially effective in consequence. But there can be little doubt that the prevalent view among the seculars—that the old Church was still alive among them—was the idea which retained many of the laity in adhesion to the faith and which procured many conversions. What did men suppose was the nature of the Church to which they gave their loyalty?

At the most immediate level of experience there can be little doubt that it was the retention of the Mass which, for most, characterized Catholicism. In the Western Rising of 1549 the leaders called for 'the sacrament hung over the high altar, and thus to be worshipped as it was wont to be'. In the reign of Elizabeth it was Mass vestments and vessels, which the 'Church papists' kept hidden for clandestine use and in hope of a public restoration. For many there must have been a large deposit of inarticulate instinct in their adhesion to the Mass. Few could have understood what went on at the altar or thought it necessary to do so: they attended to say their prayers in the presence of a mystery from which they believed they could benefit without active participation. This must have heightened, if anything, their sense of loss when the State Church Holy Communion service, in the English tongue, removed the mysterious and sacrificial content from the rite. The appeal of the miraculous was evident in other surviving Catholic practices. The visit of a priest to the house of the gentry would sometimes be the occasion for faith healings or blessings, and for exorcisms. The retention of pre-Reformation fast and feast days by Elizabethan Catholics not only served to distinguish them from their Protestant neighbours but were often in themselves associated with quasi-miraculous popular devotional legacies. The use by the Mary Ward sisters of York of holy medals blessed by the Pretender,

Charles III, to cure the 'King's Evil', as late as the end of the eighteenth century, is sometimes cited as evidence of lingering Jacobite sympathy: it is also an indication of the miraculous appeal of folk Catholicism. The popularity of the Holy Well of St Winifrid in Flintshire, to which Catholic pilgrimages continued throughout these years and well into modern times, is also testimony to an appeal not satisfied by the cool rationality of Anglicanism. In 1686 James II visited the well to pray; it had remained open even during the lean years of the Commonwealth.

Amongst the more learned who retained or were converted to the old faith there seems to have been one particularly decisive consideration: the sense of belonging to a universal society whose truths were inseparable from the religious institution in which they were conveyed. Theirs was basically a rejection of the central claim of Anglicanism—that a national Church was competent, without reference to the rest of Christendom, to determine doctrine. It was for this Catholic belief that St John Fisher and St Thomas More had died in 1535. At his trial More had declared that no individual church could legislate for the whole body; his was a vision of the unity of the Church. One of the purposes of the Pilgrimage of Grace had been 'to have the supreme head, touching *cura animarum*, to be reserved unto the See of Rome, as before it was accustomed to be'. The Marian Catholic bishops had declined to take part in the parliamentary discussion of Elizabeth's religious settlement on the grounds that religious truth could not be determined by Acts of Parliament. The sense that Christianity entailed membership of a universal body and was properly independent of local political control was an enduring part of the appeal of Catholicism to subsequent converts. It lay at the heart of Newman's adhesion to the Church in 1845. But this idea did not involve papalism: the Catholics of Elizabeth's reign were staunch Englishmen who retained that suspicion of Roman authority which had characterized medieval English Catholicism. Even More had argued that General Councils of the Church were superior to the Pope. There had been no agreement about the extent or nature of papal jurisdiction in the English Catholicism of the past, and Elizabethan Catholics did not rush to assert the primacy of the Pope as a counter to the Erastianism of the new State Church. The Jesuits tended to higher views of papal powers than others: they were centred in Rome and derived their claims to exemption from the jurisdiction of the seculars from papal authority. Queen Mary had resisted the authority of Rome in her protection of Cardinal Pole and in her insistence that any action against him would have to proceed in English ecclesiastical courts, not in Roman ones. This resistance to papal jurisdiction was clearly not incompatible with acknowledgement of the Pope's spiritual authority and with a sense that it guaranteed the essential unity of Christendom; but it was a real enough element in post-Reformation English Catholicism, influencing the secular clergy in their desire for government by bishops rather than for a continuation of the direct authority of Rome exercised by Propaganda. The 'Gallicanism' which nineteenth-century ultramontane bishops attributed to the control of the English Church by the gentry for two-and-a-half centuries was actually of medieval origin.

The English Reformation occurred in circumstances of religious fluidity, of a ferment of ideas for change. When the dividing lines were drawn men of very similar intellectual and spiritual outlooks found themselves on opposite sides: the lines were drawn for political and national considerations, and the religious consequences were intended to fall into place according to the principle of *cuius regio, eius religio*. But the Catholic minority who found themselves outside the Elizabethan settlement did not suddenly jettison the English religious attitudes they had inherited, and the lines were still quite easily crossed and recrossed. Priests like Anthony Tyrell, once chaplain to Lord Vaux, changed allegiance between Protestant and Catholic several times; leading bishops alternated—Cranmer, Latimer, Tunstall, and Gardiner had all done so. This was not a lack of integrity, a bowing to the wind. It was an indication of the real difficulty men felt when seeking to adapt an incoherent and idiosyncratic religious tradition to an emergent intellectual and spiritual culture which demanded clear formulations and precise allegiances. A few, it is true, hedged their bets. Lord Stourton kept two Catholic priests in his house so that he could be reconciled to the Church at his last hour. Unhappily for him it came (in 1588) when both were away. In the next century Lady Falkland managed to conceal her conversion to Catholicism from her Protestant husband for fourteen years. Very many—probably the overwhelming majority—did not regard the Elizabethan settlement as involving fundamental religious questions and were happy to conform to the

new Church in the belief that it was in some sense a continuation of
the old one. The external order of Anglicanism, with its dignitaries
and formality, and its possession of the ancient ecclesiastical
structures, was not too radical a departure from the familiar.
Catholic worship in the difficult circumstances in which it was
offered must have been equally austere. For most Englishmen, the
fact that the bulk of the parochial clergy conformed to the new
services must have been good enough reason for regarding the
settlement as a reform and not a revolution. Anglicanism appeared to
many to have no specific statement of doctrine which could divide
men: there was no equivalent of the Augsburg Confession or the
Heidelberg Catechism or the Decrees of the Council of Trent. There
was little public reaction to the changes and most men 'unawares to
themselves', as the Benedictine Augustine Baker wrote, 'became
neutrals in religion'. Their children accepted the new order as part of
the ordinary background of things, and it was to them that the
mission priests after 1574 directed their message of a distinct
Catholicism. The tiny minority of Englishmen who had throughout
adhered to the old faith, however, had a very clear sense of its
continuity with the past: they formed the link to the future, and
whether their priority was retention of the Mass or a sense of
belonging to a universal body (or family loyalty, social deference,
innate conservatism or superstition), they felt that they were at one
with preceding English religion. Some gave their lives for that
conviction.

    The extent to which the English Catholics discriminated between
the spiritual jurisdiction of the papacy and other papal claims to
authority was demonstrated in their protestations of loyalty to the
Crown. 'I confessed an obedience due to the Crown as my temporal
head and primate,' Campion said at his trial; 'I will willingly pay to
her Majesty what is hers, yet I must pay to God what is his.' Sir
Thomas Tresham, despite heavy fines and long imprisonment, swore
to defend Elizabeth and the realm from all invasion by 'Prince, pope,
or potentate'. Some were prepared to go a long way in opposition to
papal authority in order to show their English national self-
consciousness and their loyalty—the long disputes in the seventeenth century among Catholics themselves about the propriety of
taking loyalty oaths in which papal powers were explicitly denied
were evidence of this. Thirteen priests signed a Protestation of

Allegiance in 1603 which appeared to denounce papal authority in rather more than merely temporal matters. It was presented shortly before the death of the Queen. This was actually within a pattern of response established by the situation forced upon the English Catholics by the bull of 1570. Few had felt the Pope had any real competence in the political sphere, and doubtless many resented the intolerable jeopardy in which their loyalty was placed through what became known as the 'Bloody Question': would they defend the realm against an invasion sanctioned by the Pope? A new oath of allegiance in 1606 denounced the papal claim to a deposing power as 'impious and heretical', yet a number of Catholic priests took it. Among them was George Blackwell, who was deposed from his office of Archpriest by the papacy in consequence. In 1611 his successor, George Birkhead, pronounced the excommunication of all those priests who had taken the oath. In 1634, on a visit to Oxford, the President of the English Benedictine Congregation, Dom Leander de Sancto Martino (whose name, in the world, was Jack Jones, and who came from Brecon), advised the English Catholics not to publish books which exaggerated papal authority. In the tradition of Allen and Parsons, however, there was a continuing minority of English Catholics, mostly resident on the Continent, who espoused the cause of armed force to change the political situation in their country. It was awareness of this tradition which enabled successive governments to renew the penal legislation and to keep alive popular suspicions of Catholic disloyalty. There can be little doubt that most Catholics preferred the civil disabilities and physical deprivations of the Protestant administration to the conquest of their land by the Spanish or the French. St Henry Walpole declared his love of England from his prison cell in 1595: for 'peace, moral virtue and good government' his own land was beyond comparison.

There is no way of knowing how many Catholics there were in the reign of Elizabeth—there was no clear line between 'Church papists' and recusants when it came to interior conviction. Recusancy convictions and fines were too haphazardly procured to be any guidance. But the picture became clearer in the seventeenth century. The numbers of clergy available to serve the Catholic community is also no reliable indication of its total size since fluctuations depended in some measure upon the relative severity of public policy. At the end of the sixteenth century there were probably some 300 priests in

England, and by the end of the eighteenth century there were around 400. Between these dates there had been a peak, at around the middle years of the reign of Charles I, of some 750 priests. They were very unevenly distributed since their base was not the parochial unit but the gentry house which harboured them. In the first half of the seventeenth century there were perhaps 40,000 Catholics in England and Wales. Their numbers had quietly expanded during the later years of Elizabeth, as the mission priests began to restore an effective presence, and continued to do so until the second half of the seventeenth century, when they probably stabilized. Expansion began again early in the eighteenth century and continued right up until the great Irish immigration of the nineteenth century transformed the Church. A parliamentary return of 1767 showed a Catholic population of 69,376, but this was rather less than the real figure, which was around 80,000. The balance between secular and regular clergy shifted from time to time, but by the mid-seventeenth century there were probably slightly more seculars, despite the considerable increase of English religious houses on the Continent early in the century. The English Catholic Church, therefore, was not to be regarded—as it sometimes was by the nineteenth-century ultramontanes anxious to exult in their own effectiveness—as a decaying structure subject to more or less permanent erosion, but as quietly expanding slightly ahead of ordinary population growth until the mid-seventeenth century, then static, and then increasing again at a rate roughly corresponding to population increase in general.

It is difficult to categorize English Catholicism under the penal laws, partly because its institutional dislocation produced abnormal distortions of its nature, and partly because it anyway did not correspond to conventional classifications. The community which existed in the gentry houses and among their dependants, and the surviving small numbers of urban Catholics, did not constitute a 'denomination', since denominational status requires a public relationship to other religious groups and to society in general which simply did not exist. Catholics, anyway, only very slowly came to have what may be called a 'denominational' outlook on their social fate, and this did not emerge, to the extent that it emerged at all, until the nineteenth century. Nor was the community a 'sect'. In the typology usually adopted within the sociology of religion membership of a sect is exclusive in the sense that individuals opt for it through some sort of conversion experience; and a sect is a religion of the poor and the socially disinherited. Parsons and Campion certainly cultivated an evangelical search for spiritual purity of worship and Christian life which had suggestions of sectarianism, but most Catholics who re-emerged in the reign of Elizabeth were born into the faith or adopted it in circumstances where hereditary Catholicism was usual. Though 'disinherited' in the most literal sense, Catholicism had no apocalyptic or millennial overtones and could not be classified as a 'religion of the poor'. It was, on the contrary, for two hundred years largely a church of the gentry and their clients. Probably most Catholics consciously regarded their condition as abnormal, and awaited the change of political and dynastic fortunes which would lead to a national restoration of the faith. If that was the case, then the Catholic presence in England can be firmly categorized as 'Church' type—a Church undergoing internal exile, as it were, but a body nevertheless preserving memories of inclusive institutional machinery, and preparing itself to emerge into more normal relationships and sacred offices when circumstances allowed.

The conditions of dislocation in which the clergy performed their duties do not seem to have caused them to redefine the nature of their calling—as, for example, happened with Protestant sectarians among the European poor of their own day, or among the frontier churches of nineteenth-century America. The English Church was financially autonomous, depending upon incomes from gentry patrons, collections made by the worshippers, and some local endowments. The colleges on the Continent got occasional and not large subsidies from the papacy and the Spanish Crown. The clergy were in general extremely poor. Their life was hard. Those accommodated in the attics of the gentry houses were perhaps the most comfortable in material terms, but it must have been a desolate existence nonetheless (a solitary life to which the Benedictines took most easily), especially when their patrons expected those with legal or other secular professional knowledge to undertake work for them. The travelling clergy, who survived right through the seventeenth century, went from house to house, changing name and dress to avoid detection by the authorities, and said Mass, preached, heard confessions, and gave spiritual direction in each place. Some of the seculars retained private incomes. In Elizabeth's time recruitment to the clergy was about equally drawn from the gentry and from other social backgrounds; this shifted in favour of the gentry sons in the first half of the seventeenth century, but in the following century the gentry element declined sharply. The social levels of those to whom they ministered is less easily summarized. The gentry dominated the organization of the Church, but most of the members were servants, tenants, and small-town artisans. Catholicism was most persistent in the uplands of the north of England and in Lancashire. In some of those areas it formed a substantial minority within local communities. It existed in small pockets in the middle western counties of the Welsh marches and in Sussex, Hampshire, and Dorset. Apart from the court Catholics in London, adherents were fewest in areas of social and economic change—in the south-east corner of England. Despite the penal laws, the Church managed to keep up its essential rites. Anglican clergy would usually enter Catholic baptisms in their parochial registers, provided the fees were paid. Catholic marriages were generally recognized up to the Marriage Act of 1753, and thereafter Catholics underwent two ceremonies, one in the Protestant parish church and one performed by their own priest. Burials sometimes involved difficulty: the Protestant clergy occasionally refused burial to Catholics, in which case bodies were interred by the roadside or in some nearby place. In general, however, Catholics buried their dead in the parochial churchyards at night. There could be no public worship except in time of relaxation of the penal laws, and even then it could not (apart from the Embassy Chapels in London) be performed in ecclesiastical buildings. Yet Mass was said throughout the country through all those years. Catholicism survived.

3 Catholics under the penal laws

During the reigns of the first two Stuart kings the position of the English Catholics improved considerably; during the reigns of the second two, many of the gains were lost. The impression of an actual expansion of Catholicism in the later years of James I is probably deceptive: the relative relaxation of the penal laws allowed existing recusants a greater confidence, and it led also to a preparedness by those who had kept their Catholicism hidden to adopt a public profession. James himself seemed anxious to avoid further action against the Catholics—his wife, Anne of Denmark, had been secretly reconciled to the Church—but was overtaken by events. The Bye Plot in 1603 was inspired by a Catholic priest, and others were believed to have been involved, and all of the Gunpowder Plot organizers in 1605 were Catholics. Four Jesuits were identified by the Government as linked to the Plot, including Henry Garnet the Superior of the Jesuits in England. He was executed, as were the others suspected of involvement, and in the ensuing tightening of the penal laws many Catholics went into exile overseas to avoid persecution. Two new Acts in 1606 imposed an annual sacramental test for public office and a revised oath of allegiance, and restricted recusants' internal movement in the country and closed many of the professions to Catholics. The new oath was condemned by Pope Paul V, yet a number of priests had taken it. It declared that the papacy had no political authority in England, but its phrasing was sufficiently inclusive to suggest that all papal jurisdiction was incompatible with the claims of the Crown upon its subjects. During the reign, seventeen priests and six lay Catholics were executed; and in the early years of the succeeding reign the rigour of the law was still applied to Catholics (of whom the most revered was St Edmund Arrowsmith, martyred in Lancashire in 1628). As under Elizabeth, however, the Government was as much concerned with extreme Protestant threats to the religious settlement as it was with the

Catholics: in 1612 the last burning of heretics in England took place—of an Anabaptist and an Arian. Popular dislike of Catholicism continued, and was doubtless heightened by the Gunpowder Plot. The Jesuits had by now entered deeply into the national demonology, and the widespread sense that there were too many secret Catholics at work in court circles was reinforced by public antipathy to the King's proposals for a Spanish marriage for his heir. Yet the last dozen or so years of the King's reign, up to 1625, were ones of relative repose for the Catholic community. The penal legislation, once again, was allowed to exist in abeyance in many parts of the country, and even the new restrictions on the professions were not observed rigorously. At the end of the reign there were some eighty Catholic Justices of the Peace, and two High Sheriffs; and in 1624 the Protestant Archbishop Abbot of Canterbury observed that Catholics 'go by the thousand to mass'.

This stable position was inherited by Charles I and continued. The penal laws were even less systematically applied: indeed, visitors to London were impressed by the public displays of Catholicism in court circles and by the ease with which Catholic worship could be conducted. Recusancy fines continued to be exacted—usually from the lesser gentry rather than the nobility or the better-connected higher country gentlemen—for the fines now constituted a regular means of income for the Government. Charles himself was loyal to Anglicanism, and insisted on Anglican baptism for the son born in 1630, despite the marriage treaty with France which stipulated that the royal children were to be brought up as Catholics. The King's marriage to Henrietta Maria, of course, was one of the most useful aids the Catholics had. Her Catholicism, though extremely distasteful to the people of the country in general, was expressed with an exuberance which not only enhanced Catholic morale but provided protection for the public reappearance of Catholic worship. Her household originally consisted of a French Catholic bishop and twenty-seven priests; this, after objections in the Government, was reduced to twelve Catholic chaplains. The Chapel Royal in St James's became a Catholic centre, to which aristocratic converts resorted in some numbers. Most of the new Catholic peers of the reign were the result of the Stuart practice of selling titles of nobility, however, rather than from conversions, but the new respectability of court Catholicism did have the effect of reducing secessions to

Protestantism among the noble families. Public disapproval of the Catholicism of the court, which became an ingredient in the antipathy between the King and Parliament, was aggravated by Henrietta Maria's offering of prayers at Tyburn in 1626 in honour of the Catholic martyrs who had died there. The situation was not an unmixed blessing for Catholicism, either. A discernible rift began to appear between court Catholicism, with its cosmopolitanism and its greater openness to the triumphalist atmosphere of the Tridentine Church, and the country Catholics in the houses of the squires with their, by now, established habits of discretion and their insistence on their own Englishness in worship.

The foundation of the New World colony of Maryland in 1634 by Lord Baltimore (who had become a Catholic in 1625) was a further sign of Catholic advance. It was intended as a Catholic refuge, and soon had a few Jesuit priests as ministers to the settlers. The colony also illustrated an important characteristic of English Catholicism —its tenacity in less economically and socially developed parts of the country. For the Maryland settlement was a careful attempt to reproduce a quasi-manorial system which had just passed away in England itself. Maryland was a work of social as well as religious restoration. In 1692 the comparative freedom of Catholics there came to an end: the Church of England was established by law and penal legislation against Catholicism was introduced.

Another sign of the better position of Catholicism under Charles I was the resumption of diplomatic, if informal, contacts with the Holy See. In 1633 Sir Robert Douglas began to reside in Rome as representative of Henrietta Maria. He had the sanction of the King, who clearly looked for some sort of channel of communication with the Pope. Thereafter a succession of papal agents arrived in London: Dom Leander de Sancto Martino and Gregorio Panzani in 1634, and then George Con and Carlo Rossetti, the last of whom left in 1641 at the insistence of Parliament. These contacts were encouraged, on the English side, not primarily in the hope of easing the lot of the Catholics but in order to achieve some link, however slight, with the European diplomacy of the Holy See. But the Catholics were also beneficiaries of the improved relationships all round, and showed their gratitude in the Civil War. Although it is true that during the war most Catholics, like most Englishmen in general, avoided taking sides between the King and Parliament, many leading Catholic gentlemen came out in active support of Charles. For some, no doubt, this loyalism reflected continued proof of the declarations of allegiance which they and their predecessors had made since the start of the Elizabethan settlement; for some it was inspired by a desire to maintain the religious peace they had enjoyed under the King. Catholic aristocrats flocked to the court at Oxford. When Basing House, a celebrated stronghold of royalism, was taken by the parliamentary forces after a siege, ten Catholic priests were found inside. In cities held by the Crown, particularly in the north of England, Catholic worship was held publicly. Yet both sides in the Civil War continued, in appropriate circumstances, to exact recusant fines: an indication of the extent to which they had become an almost conventional form of taxation.

The balance of option between Crown and Parliament must still in some cases have been a fine one for some Catholics. From neither, since the Reformation, had Catholicism received much benefit —rather the reverse—and although the greater preparedness of Parliament to impose still harsher penal laws obviously made them the greater evil in a material sense, there must have been many gentry Catholics who felt an ideological sympathy for some of the parliamentarians' constitutional and natural law claims. It was probably realism, however, which prompted Lord Brudenell and Lord Arundell to attempt some sort of arrangement between the Catholics and the Protectorate government, just before the death of Cromwell in 1658. Thomas White (known in his literary name as Blacklo) had also urged the Catholic clergy to come to terms with the Protectorate; and St John Southworth, executed by the Commonwealth, had declared his loyalty to the republican government on the scaffold. The Catholic Sir Kenelm Digby had performed diplomatic services overseas for Cromwell. The parliamentarians had at first reinforced the penal laws where they had the opportunity to do so, and eleven Catholic priests were executed in 1641-2. There were further executions up to 1646, but enforcement of the laws was then made less strict, and between 1647 and 1660 only two priests were sent to their deaths. Charles I had himself consented to a reimposition of the laws after 1638, in order to offset the impression, widespread among his opponents, that a formal Catholic restoration was in some way in preparation. Under the Rump Parliament in 1650 the Act requiring compulsory attendance at church was repealed—but this was intended as an assault upon the Anglicans and not as a relief to the Catholics. 'Popery and prelacy' were explicitly excluded from the declaration of religious liberty made under the Commonwealth. There was a single Oath of Abjuration which was more anti-Catholic in its language and demands than previous oaths of supremacy to the Crown. Government during the Interregnum persisted in equating Catholicism and royalism.

The Catholics therefore expected much of the restoration of the Stuart monarchy when it came in 1660. Charles II had himself, during his exile, frequently shown favour to Catholics at his court, and was personally grateful to them for assisting his escape from England. His actual policy was to give as much toleration as he could to Catholicism in conjunction with equal liberty for Protestant Dissenters: hence the Declaration of Breda, which so encouraged Catholics in their hopes of the restored monarchy, by its promise of freedom of conscience 'for differences of opinion in matters of religion which do not disturb the peace of the kingdom'. In the Secret Treaty of Dover, between Charles II and Louis XIV of France, furthermore, there was provision for the King to make a public adoption of Catholicism. In 1662 he married a Catholic, Catharine of Braganza. But it was not until his death, in 1685, that Charles was received into the Catholic Church—by Fr. John Huddleston, the priest who had assisted his escape from Worcester. His attempt to help the Catholics came with the Declaration of Indulgence in 1672, but when he met parliamentary opposition he drew back. The legislation at the start of the reign, which was intended to clarify the nature of the old religious settlement as restored after the ravages of the Interregnum, and which was known collectively as the Clarendon Code, was primarily intended to contain the influence of the Puritans, but Catholics suffered equally through its restrictions. Clarendon himself was not an anti-Catholic. Twice in 1660 he expressed the belief that the English Catholics should be allowed a bishop of their own. But his priority was a Church settlement acceptable to the Presbyterians, and satisfying the Catholics was not allowed to interfere with this. By the terms of the Corporation Act in 1661 local office-holders had to receive the Anglican sacrament annually; the Act of Uniformity in 1662 deprived incumbents in the State Church who refused to conform to the Prayer Book; under the Conventicle Act of 1664 no more than four persons were allowed to assemble for non-Anglican worship; the Five Mile Act of 1665 restricted the movements of Dissenting clergy and imposed strict licensing on schoolteachers. In addition to impediments resulting from the Code, Catholics had also to face all the restrictions and inconveniences of the old penal laws. These, however, were, once again, in general held *in terrorem*. Recusancy returns of 1671 showed that only half the counties appeared to have enforced the laws at all, and that even in them there were large-scale exemptions for prominent local Catholics and fines fixed at low levels for others. Court Catholicism flourished, much to the alarm of some Anglicans, and with the restoration of the Dukedom of Norfolk to the Howards in 1661 it was plain that prominent Catholic families could look with some confidence to the Restoration.

Yet most of these early blossoms were to wither on the branch. In 1673 Parliament showed its unpreparedness to tolerate prerogative government by the Crown when it passed the Test Act in a direct repudiation of the King's Declaration of Indulgence. The Act not only circumvented the attempt to suspend the anti-Catholic laws but it added still more to the list, requiring a sacramental test and a declaration against Transubstantiation from office-holders. In 1678 a second Test Act removed Catholics from the House of Lords. Catholics had been excluded from the Commons since the Act of 1563; now their formal removal from the Lords produced a complete severance from government. From this point the Catholics ran into increasing trouble with Parliament and with public opinion, and then, in a heightened atmosphere of hostility, came the notorious 'Popish Plot' of 1678. Even the Great Fire of London, in 1666, had been popularly blamed on the Catholics: mobs had burned the Pope in effigy. Andrew Marvell's *Account of the Growth of Popery and Arbitrary Government*—its very title summarizing the suspicions that the court and the Catholics were inherently given to the imposition of an autocracy—also loaded the Catholics with responsibility for the conflagration in London. The tract was written in 1677 and circulated the next year. It rehearsed all kinds of horror stories about papal deposing powers and popish superstition, and both reflected and stimulated the excited condition of opinion. The real existence of fringe conspiracies among small groups of uninfluential Catholics cannot be denied, but the Popish Plot, when it burst upon England, was out of all proportion. Yet the revelations of Titus Oates attracted widespread belief among all sections of society. Oates himself had been expelled from three schools and rusticated from Cambridge, but apparently had no difficulty in being ordained in the Church of England. He had then been converted to Catholicism and studied for the priesthood at Valladolid. After expulsion from that college, he returned to his Anglican allegiance and became an anti-Catholic informer. His revelations of a deeply laid Catholic plot against the Constitution, and the death in unexplained circumstances of the magistrate to whom he had made some of his depositions—which was blamed on the Jesuits—elicited something like national hysteria. Parliament reinforced the penal laws and the worst persecution of Catholics since the reign of Elizabeth began. Oates himself was found guilty of perjury in 1685, and died as a member of the Baptist Church in 1705. Catholic deaths preceded his. About a hundred clergy were arrested altogether (perhaps a sixth of those in England), and of these seventeen were executed and twenty-three died in prison. The work both of the Church and of the Society of Jesus was set back by years. Eleven of the forty Catholic peers were imprisoned for treason: Stafford was executed and Lord Petre died in the Tower. Finally, in 1681, St Oliver Plunket, Archbishop of Armagh, was put to death at Tyburn—the last priest to die for his religion in England.

The country slowly recovered from the anti-Catholic frenzy; yet still the Whigs' insistence on linking popery and absolutist government was demonstrated in the Exclusion crisis. But James II succeeded to the throne in 1685. His Catholicism, however, was not in such circumstances to be a help to the Catholics, whose initial euphoria once more proved short-lived. James's coronation in Westminster Abbey was according to the rites of the Church of England, and for his first year little was done to suggest that the position of the Catholics was to be ameliorated. Then, in 1686, began what to opponents looked like an attempt at a Catholic restoration: and it was, as with his predecessor, use of royal prerogative powers to effect religious changes which most alarmed Anglicans and Englishmen in general. The inspiration of the King's new policy was not Fr. Edward Petre, the Jesuit conventionally attributed with political influence over James II, but the King himself and the Earl of Sunderland. Catholics were given senior appointments in the universities—John Massey, in a particularly insensitive move, was intruded into the Deanery of Christ Church. Thirteen Catholics, including Petre, were appointed to the Council. Commissions in the army were granted to Catholics and four others were made judges. All over England Catholics opened chapels for public worship, in emulation of the Royal Catholic Chapel James had set up in London. In 1687 and 1688 he issued Declarations of Indulgence in an attempt to by-pass Parliament in dispensing with the anti-Catholic penal laws: seven Anglican prelates who objected were upheld by the courts. But the Government remained firmly Protestant and Anglican at all levels, and the number of Catholics in the country, the beneficiaries of this constitutional upheaval, remained exceedingly small. James, who had become accustomed to autocratic acts of kingship during the long years of exile in France, seemed unaware of how narrow his basis of power was. The result was his return to exile in the 'Glorious Revolution' of 1688, and a massive set-back for the English Catholics. Three of the Vicars Apostolic and a few priests were arrested, though they were later released after short sojourns in gaol; up to about fifty fled abroad, as did a large number of Catholic nobles and gentlemen. The exiled court at St Germain harboured several hundred of these Catholics, and the Church in England was depleted of some of its most influential supporters. The penal laws were vigorously re-enforced, and this tended to the financial ruination of the Catholic gentry who remained in England—a class that was anyway in decline during the Restoration period. A further legacy of James II's religious policy was the resuscitation of the popular culture of anti-Catholicism, and the association of adhesion to Protestantism with the preservation of political liberty. It was an ideological link which was to dog the steps of English Catholicism for a couple of centuries.

Anti-Catholic legislation continued to accumulate under William III. The Disabling Act of 1695 excluded Catholics from large areas of the legal profession, and this more or less completed the removal of Catholics from public life. Gentry domination of the Church continued despite the continued decline of that class, and despite the double land tax imposed on Catholics in 1692. Registration of Catholic lands began in 1716 as an aid to collection. The laws against priests were still sometimes enforced: in 1714 Bonaventure Giffard, the leading bishop of the time, recorded that he had had to change his lodgings fourteen times in five months to escape arrest. Yet some things continued fairly normally: at the end of the seventeenth century there were many Catholic booksellers and publishers in England, and small local Catholic schools existed throughout the Catholic areas in the land. The reign of George II was the first since the Elizabethan settlement in which no new laws against Catholicism were passed. By then, however, gentry control of the Church was slipping away, with the rise of semi-autonomous urban congregations, and the old Catholic nobility was noticeably depleted. There were only seven Catholic peers left by the last decade of the eighteenth century: in some families there had been a failure of heirs; in many there had been defections to Protestantism. The Dukes of Norfolk, Beaufort, Bolton, and Richmond had all left the Church. The lingering popular association of Catholicism and Jacobitism probably assisted the apostasies. Catholic support for the Stuarts was actually in decline quite early in the eighteenth century, though this was disguised by public belief that Catholics had organized the 1715 Rising. Two Catholic peers, Lord Derwentwater and Lord Widdrington, were executed for their involvement. A number of Catholic priests and laymen were also arrested after the 1745 Rebellion, and several chapels were destroyed by mobs in Lancashire. But the Catholics were not greatly affected by the Rebellion, and excitement soon passed—an indication of their real distance, by that date, from Jacobite activism. The clergy formally adhered to the Stuarts all the time that Rome did, although the belief expressed early in the century by a few, like John Stonor and Thomas Strickland, that Catholics should declare their loyalty to the Hanoverians, was slowly gaining ground. Mass was offered in many places for the success of Prince Charles Edward in 1745; but when the papacy ended its support for Stuart claims, on the death of the Old Pretender, James III, in 1765, prayers at Mass were switched at once to George III.

It is difficult to assess the real influence of Rome over the English Catholic Church between the Elizabethan settlement and the middle years of the eighteenth century. There were obviously variations from time to time, but government of the Church directly by the papacy—through the actual direction of the central missionary agency in Rome, the Sacred Congregation of Propaganda—secured a more effective control of such policy as there was than the apparent incoherence of gentry management on the ground in England might at first sight indicate. It was broadly true that from the middle years of Elizabeth onwards (and fairly consistently) the secular clergy sought a release from missionary status and a return to normal canonical ecclesiastical administration under diocesan bishops, whereas the regular orders, and especially the Jesuits, preferred the flexibility and freedom from episcopal control inherent in missionary status. These two centuries were to see numerous disputes among the English clergy about this central issue. The seculars regarded themselves as a continuation of the medieval Church, and held still to a fully territorial view of their ministry, regarding the times as untypical and awaiting the return of normality; the Jesuits, by the time the English Province was set up in 1623, saw England as a more or less permanent missionary area. These rival views were complicated by another consideration: whether England should be governed according to the Decrees of the Council of Trent. The restoration of a formal hierarchy of bishops would not be a straightforward return to the practice of the past, because the Catholic Church which England had known in the past had been superseded by the Tridentine model. There were differences of view about how the necessary adaptations should be made. Pro-Catholic sovereigns like Charles II and James II favoured canonical bishops, since a church under local episcopal control was more easily managed according to Crown preferences than one governed by Propaganda. In 1686, 1696, and 1703 there were papal decisions in favour of the seculars' claim that the regular clergy could only operate with their authorization—the actual question around which the ideological differences in practice turned—and in the Brief *Apostolicum Ministerium* of Benedict XIV, in 1753, which governed the organization of the Church in England until the restoration of the hierarchy in 1850, the seculars' general view of the Church was upheld.

After the Elizabethan settlement, Rome had at first vacillated and then, when it had become clear that a Catholic presence persisted in England, an Archpriest had been appointed to take charge of the English Catholics. Disputes between the seculars and the regulars, in the 'stirs' at Wisbech and in the English College at Rome, had already shown the need for some sort of discipline to be reestablished. The office of Archpriest was without precedent in England, and the first to be placed in it, in 1598, faced unprecedented problems. George Blackwell was appointed to govern with twelve assistants, under the authority of the nuncio in Brussels. His partiality for the Jesuits, however, led to immediate suspicions among the secular priests that the new system of ecclesiastical government was intended to further the Society's conception of the Church in England, as a permanent mission. Blackwell had been directed to consult formally with the Superior of the Jesuits. The result was the rise of the 'Appellants', a group of secular clergy who appealed to Rome in 1600 against Blackwell's authority, and in favour of an oath of allegiance to the English Crown which would explicitly accept papal spiritual jurisdiction but eschew any temporal claims. In this they sought an ultimate return to government by ordinary bishops; in the short term they procured the dismissal of Blackwell by the Pope in 1607 for having subscribed a very comparable oath. The Roman authorities tried a new scheme of government for England in 1623, with the appointment of William Bishop as Vicar Apostolic (with the rank of Bishop and the titular see, *in partibus infidelium*, of Chalcedon). It was an arrangement which was to endure, despite an intermission between 1631 and 1685, until the mid-nineteenth-century restoration of the hierarchy. Bishop's tenure of office was a brief nine months, but before his death he set up an informal Chapter of the clergy and an outline structure of Church government under twenty archdeacons, and he came to an amicable arrangement with the Benedictines whereby their mission priests had a recognized degree of autonomy. His successor, Bishop Richard Smith, arrived in London in 1625 and toured the country to see conditions for himself. Disputes again surfaced: Smith sought to bring some sort of coherence to the finances of the mission and, with the support of Propaganda, tried to arrange that donations for the upkeep of the clergy should be made through the archdeacons rather than directly by patrons. He also claimed jurisdiction in matrimonial and testamentary cases, and over the regulars' right to officiate. This upset both the gentry, who saw the prospect of losing their control of the clergy they paid for, and the regular clergy, who were unprepared to surrender their autonomy. Some Catholic gentry petitioned the Privy Council against his authority, a warrant for his arrest was issued, and in 1631 Smith fled to France, where he lived until his death in 1658, still technically in office. His career was a clear attempt to preserve the notion of the English mission as a survivor of the pre-Reformation Catholic Church awaiting formal reconstitution. By the mid-seventeenth century there were almost as many regular clergy as seculars in England, however, so Smith's complaint about the 'harassing regulars' was not against an influential but minority body, but against a half of the Church. Panzani's mission to London as special papal agent in 1634 had been intended to effect a reconciliation of the seculars and regulars; but in this he was not successful, for their rivalries were not about mere matters of overlapping jurisdiction but about fundamental differences of view over the nature of the Catholic Church in England. The weakness of the Church was exacerbated by decentralization, and the quarrels of the seculars and regulars prevented the establishment of effective machinery to offset it.

The authority of the Chapter of the secular clergy set up in 1623 was not formally recognized by Propaganda, but in practice it exercised some sort of jurisdiction through the archdeacons until it declined into a self-perpetuating benevolent society in the eighteenth century. It also kept alive the idea of a continuous Church, and in the person of Thomas White (known also as Blacklo) it had an influential if unorthodox supporter. White came originally from Essex, and was educated at the Jesuit school at St Omer and the English College at Valladolid, and finally at Douai. In 1624 he studied in Paris. After some years in the European colleges he returned to England in 1667 where, having by then turned against the Jesuits and having espoused a complicated set of attitudes to Catholic authority which amounted to a kind of Jansenism, he dominated the Chapter. He was by any standards a distinguished scholar, wrote over forty works, and was a friend of Hobbes. 'Blackloism' was an attempt to restate Catholicism within the canons of prevalent intellectual attitudes; it was critical of the universal claims of the papacy. In practical English terms, White supported the Chapter's vision of a restored hierarchy. He died in 1676, regarded by many English Catholics as a deeply unsound sceptic of received Catholic values. His influence on the Chapter was matched by that of another remarkable man. John Sergeant was originally a High Church Anglican who had become a Catholic during the Civil War. He was secretary to the Chapter from 1653, and produced a series of defences of the seculars' claim to be the successors of the medieval English Church. In 1673 he left England in the belief that the Jesuits were plotting against him, and although he later returned, a lot of the seculars' confidence in their ancient claims had by then slipped away.

The rule of the Vicars Apostolic returned with Bishop John Leyburn, a former President of Douai, in 1685. He was a man of moderate judgement who avoided political involvements and who knew the condition of the English mission well—having once been chaplain to Lord Montague. His appointment was greeted with some reservation by the Chapter, who persisted in their hope of a canonical episcopate. Leyburn prepared the division of Catholic England into four districts, each to be under a separate Vicar Apostolic, and this structure was carried into effect, with the approval of James II and to the dismay of the Chapter, in 1688. Leyburn himself retained the London District, Bonaventure Giffard was appointed by Rome to the Midland District, James Smith went to the Northern District, and Dom Michael Ellis to the Western District (which was normally thereafter to be held by a regular). Rural Deans were appointed in each District as well. It was an arrangement which endured until the mid-nineteenth century. James II intended to endow each of the Districts with a grant of £1,000 per annum; his exile prevented the benefaction. But the Vicars Apostolic were consecrated in royal palaces. An important break with the past had occurred: the boundaries of the Districts did not correspond to any of the ancient sees or provinces, and the creation of the new ecclesiastical units was a frank recognition of the missionary nature of English Catholicism. It was not, in the circumstances, surprising that the Chapter clergy objected to the new arrangements. Leyburn himself was arrested during the Glorious Revolution of 1688, imprisoned in the Tower, and released after two years. He governed the London District until his death in 1702, and was succeeded by Giffard.

The English Catholic Church in the eighteenth century produced some strange paradoxes: cut off from the national life more or less completely by the penal laws, it nevertheless showed an increasing proximity to the values of the times; removed from the influence of general European Catholicism by its missionary nature and its gentry localism, it still emerged at the end of the century with the first signs of a Roman orientation among the clergy. Both externally and internally the Church came to have a number of common features with the Protestantism around it. The new Catholic chapels that were built in the mid-century and afterwards—the first free-standing buildings, outside the gentry houses—were indistinguishable from contemporaneous Dissenting chapels. In many there were box-pews, some with fees. There was an absence of statues, votive lights, or almost any other ornament. Incense was rare, and so was reservation of the Blessed Sacrament and devotions to the saints. The atmosphere of the religion within was also peculiarly adapted to the Age of Reason: the emphasis was on benevolence, just as in the eighteenth-century Anglican Church, and the tone was pietistic. Popular preaching, especially in the growing numbers of urban chapels, was also marked by a moral earnestness usually thought characteristic of the Protestantism of the period. Educated Catholics, even conservative ones like Bishop Challoner, had an antipathy to any devotional practice that looked 'superstitious', and they emphasized the scriptural basis of Christian teaching. After the mid-century, exorcisms and faith healings became rare and relics were stored away—not to reappear until the ultramontanes revived a taste for them a hundred years later. Catholic worship must have seemed exceedingly bleak for the poor, who probably found the prayers in English, which spread under Challoner's influence, rather too literate for their religious senses. In some country houses, and in the Embassy Chapels in London, the splendour of worship continued, but in the new chapels the 'English' spirit seeped in as the years passed: it was this that the nineteenth-century ultramontanes reacted against. The revised Constitution of the English Benedictine Congregation, issued in 1784, removed a large number of extravagant practices—now thought more suited to southern European mentalities—and the tone of enlightenment echoed through the emptied corridors even of the monastic life. Most of the disciplines and devotional exercises now formally expunged had probably long been disused anyway, but the changes were significant.

In theological outlook, too, the spirit of the age was strongly represented. The century had opened with a lively controversy about Jansenism among the professors at Douai. It was dampened down during the long presidency of Robert Witham, from 1715 to 1738. During the second half of the century Douai again fostered an independence of mind which then became the intellectual basis of the Cisalpine spirit in English Catholicism. The central event was the expulsion of Joseph Berington from the College in 1771. Intellectual life at Douai was neither demanding or particularly inventive, and Berington's introduction of current ideas to the philosophy course was hardly revolutionary. His liberalism produced sympathetic echoes among some of the English clergy, and the laity, with their 'English' dislike of clericalism and traditional distrust of papal authority, found in his thinking about the nature of the Church a welcome openness to the realities of their society. Berington, in fact, became the most important intellectual critic of the 'superstition' of popular Catholicism. In *The State and Behaviour of the English Catholics*, published in 1780, he explicitly assailed the Catholics of Spain and Italy for unenlightened religious practices, and, in a vigorous restatement of the traditional hostility of the seculars to the regulars, he depicted the religious orders as unsuited to the progressive climate of the times. His central attack upon papal monarchy also summed up two centuries of English Catholic loyalism to the Crown. 'I am no papist,' he wrote: the Pope 'has no absolute jurisdiction over each bishop and pastor'. These opinions, of course, elicited considerable disquiet among another section of the educated Catholics—the more conservative, whose leading figure was Bishop Challoner himself. But the drift to progressive statements of Catholicism looked as if it would run over him; when the movement began for an amelioration of the penal laws it was in lay hands, and the loyalism and liberalism of Berington and those who thought like him were very much more to the taste of those who sought a place in the public life of the nation. By the 1770s some Catholics were supporters of the reformist ideas of Wilkes and of the various reform associations. Their co-operation with reform politicians for the palliation of the penal code symbolized the integration of liberal Catholicism with contemporary English culture. In the new United States, too, English Catholics demonstrated the same liberalism. Catholics had mostly supported the revolt of the thirteen colonies against Britain, and John Carroll, the first American Catholic bishop, was a progressive who favoured a vernacular liturgy and interpreted Catholic teachings as sympathetic to American ideals of political liberty. At his first synod, in 1791, he demonstrated a marked degree of independence from Roman authority. He was a defender of Berington, with whom he communicated.

Some Catholics, Berington among them, believed that their numbers were declining during the eighteenth century. But it was not so. What was declining was country-house Catholicism: the age of gentry domination of the Church was drawing to its end. It was a slow process, and was actually produced not by any significant further diminution of gentry Catholics but by the rise of an independent urban Catholicism in the towns and the new industrial centres. As yet unperceived by observers, or by themselves for that matter, Catholics of humbler social station were not only increasing in numbers but were shifting the whole centre of balance in the Church. The rise of a self-conscious Catholic middle class was beginning, urban and articulate. At the same time the clergy were becoming emanicipated from the control of the gentry patrons, and many of them, too, were now in the urban chapels, which were rapidly evolving an informal parochial structure. In their clergy associations, and through receipt of incomes donated in trusts and collections independent of the landed grandees, they were poised to take control of the Church. They were delayed by the movement for Emancipation from the penal laws, which gave the lay gentlemen an artificially extended period of dominance; but at the start of the nineteenth century the autonomy of the clergy, together with the emergence of middle-class congregations, transformed the English Church and made it more like the Protestant bodies than ever, for they, too, were in the new century to be characterized by middle-class financing and by clericalism. An early sign of the release of the Catholic clergy from gentry control was the adoption of clerical dress. By the middle years of the eighteenth century many adopted the same sort of sober dress as was worn by Dissenting ministers. The enhancement of their influence was assisted by the partial decline in the power of the regular clergy. In the mid-century, the regulars were slightly more numerous. The Benedictines alone had some 150 monks and 20 nuns in England working in the missions, and supplied by the thriving houses on the Continent. But the Jesuits, who were still the most vigorous and the most independent regulars in England, and who conducted a third of the missions, were faced with a sudden arrest of their influence in 1773, when the Society was dissolved by Clement XIV. The Vicars Apostolic, merciful in their unexpected triumph against long-standing rivals, allowed them still a considerable measure of autonomy under their own Superior, but Jesuit influence was neutralized at just the right historical moment to allow the seculars a less impeded progress to leadership over the laity. The Jesuits were not reconstituted in England until the end of the first quarter of the next century. Their passage into limbo reduced the numbers of ordinations to the priesthood, however, and that coincided with a decline in the volume of secular vocations, leading to some real shortages in the later years of the eighteenth century. The effective rule of the Vicars Apostolic was assisted by these changes. Throughout the century they had not been able to exercise any sort of joint activity, and their own common bond, indeed, was the agent they maintained in Rome. Each was independently appointed by the Holy See through the authority of the Prefect of Propaganda, and each carefully maintained his independence. It was to be the practical exigencies of the movement for Catholic Emancipation, at the very end of the century, that was to promote a co-ordinated action among them for the first time.

The shift to an urban orientation was the most profound change of the century for the Catholics. At the beginning something like two-thirds of the clergy were employed by the Catholic nobility and gentry, either in their own houses or in the early town missions (especially in places of heavy Catholic concentrations like Lancashire or Durham) under their patronage. At the end of the century perhaps three-quarters of the clergy were serving in congregational missions independent of the landed families. Had English Catholicism been as much a 'denomination' as some historians have come to contend, the domination of the gentry should have been replaced by the domination of the middle classes of the towns: they would have emerged like nineteenth-century Protestant Dissent. In Catholicism, it was the bishops who took over. The rise of episcopal control and clericalism preceded the imposition of ultramontanism: Catholicism, that is to say, reasserted its pedigree as a Church and not a denomination merely. The bulk of the Catholic urban increase was of artisans and poor men, the products of urban crafts and the Industrial Revolution. The economic transformation completed the collapse of gentry control, and it also gave the Vicars Apostolic a great degree of flexibility, since they were able to guide the expansion of chapels in areas which had never before had Catholic populations and where there was no tradition of local influence. The

Catholic Church thus had a greater capacity to adapt to the new industrial conditions than did the Church of England, which often found itself isolated in its rural strongholds and slow to accommodate to the new world that was growing up.

Despite the difficulties imposed by the penal laws, Catholic trusts in lay hands also grew, and were essential not only for the maintenance of urban chapels but also for the administration of funds for charitable purposes. The great age of humanitarian benevolence was just beginning, and Catholics were not excluded from the instincts of the time. The Moorfields chapel in London— with its external appearance of a warehouse, in accordance with the usual practice of not provoking Protestant sensibilities nor of stimulating an application of the penal laws—had a number of charities organized by a lay committee of trustees, and this was not uncommon. Early beneficiaries were the poor Irish, who were arriving on a larger scale than before, though not as yet in the massed numbers that swamped the resources of the Church in the next century. Some had always been in the English towns. In 1670 Airoldi, visiting the country as a special representative of the Holy See, had remarked that their presence in London was 'a great annoyance'. By the later decades of the eighteenth century there were several Irish districts in London, already preparing for the 'rookeries' of the nineteenth-century flood: at Wapping, Whitechapel, Holborn, Bermondsey, Southwark, and Soho. The Gordon Riots, in 1780, were most savage in the Irish districts. London Catholic organization was untypical in the sumptuous nature of public worship in the Embassy Chapels, but quite typical in the poor districts, where the new chapels were just like the ones in the new urban areas of the provinces. Eight Catholic States maintained chapels in London, and through the worst years of the penal laws they had kept a Catholic presence going. The buildings were large, and were deliberately intended to furnish public worship for the English Catholic population. Services were frequent; the Portuguese Chapel had eight Masses every Sunday. The style was baroque and triumphalist, bringing the atmosphere of the European Counter-Reformation to English worship. In that, the Embassy Chapels were unlike the ordinary missions—but like some of the eighteenth-century country-house worship. At Thorndon Hall in Essex the new chapel, opened in 1739, had regular Benediction, with a tabernacle on the altar and Catholic ornaments of a type which did not become normal in England until the rise of the 'Roman' spirit of the nineteenth century. It is as well to remember that Challoner, regarded because of his devotional writings as the great exponent of an unadorned 'Old Catholic' English style of worship, actually centred his life in London on the Sardinian Chapel at Lincoln's Inn Fields, where the liturgy was full of 'continental' splendour.

Though discreet and carefully unobtrusive, English Catholicism in the eighteenth century was not underground or hidden. Places of worship were known to the civil authorities, who chose to do nothing about them. Accounts of Mass celebrated in garrets and upper storeys of obscure inns relate more about the poverty of urban Catholics than they do about fears of prosecution or the severity of officialdom. Catholics and Protestants in general coexisted easily enough together—as seen in the *Antiquities of Hengrave*: the Gage family in Suffolk managed, despite all the paraphernalia of the law and the disapproval of opinion, to exist quite comfortably in the rural society around them. In a deferential society, Catholics of property and station were usually accorded the respect due to them, whatever the peculiarity of their religious profession. Despite the legal exclusion from the professions, which was a very real disadvantage, Catholics nevertheless emerged in public life—men like Alexander Pope, whose deism dissolved back into his early Catholicism in old age, and James Gibbs, the architect of the Senate House in Cambridge, the Radcliffe Camera in Oxford, and a number of the most noble Protestant churches in London. Education was still hindered by the law, yet Catholics crossed pretty freely to the continental English schools, and a number existed in England as well, like the Hammersmith Convent school, the Franciscan school at Edgbaston, and the Bar Convent school in York, as well as Challoner's foundations. There were Catholic booksellers, like the one consulted by Edward Gibbon prior to his conversion to Catholicism. Books were published, sometimes on the Continent and sometimes in England with false continental cities given as the imprint—a remnant of the worst years of legislative harassment. This was an emergent Church, quietly recovering the confidence of a public presence, but always sensing the possibility of a hurried return to the catacombs should the governing powers change their minds about the toleration so proudly thought to be a characteristic of the age.

The best-remembered Catholic leader of the eighteenth century was in some things strangely untypical of Catholic trends within the century as a whole. Bishop Richard Challoner certainly shared the dislike of 'superstition' so marked within educated English Catholicism, but he was very far removed from the liberalizing intellectual currents of some of his contemporaries. So far from seeking an adaptation to the Age of Reason, Challoner rather looked backwards to simpler faith and partly idealized notions of the former devotional life. His complaints about 'the great decay of piety and religion amongst a great part of our Catholics' are to be seen in this light: they assumed a passing world of Catholic uniformity which had never really been there. Challoner was not, therefore, an inventive figure, and he contributed nothing new to English Catholicism—not even, as is often supposed, a peculiarly English devotional tradition. His best-known devotional writings, and especially *The Garden of the Soul* (1740), were partly modelled upon his boyhood teacher John Gother (and his *Instructions*, a spiritual manual which endured for generations) and partly on European writing. Challoner's inspiration was much less English than it looked. He showed a proximity to European devotional styles which many have supposed absent in English Catholicism: what he did was to adapt the thought and disciplines of St Francis de Sales and St Vincent de Paul for English use, but he did not really anglicize the content. The second edition of *The Garden of the Soul* reproduced a classic of Italianate devotion: the Litany of Loretto.

Challoner's rise to leadership can hardly be said to have symptomized the emergence of middle-class Catholicism, because although he was of non-landed background, ordinations of those from the *mediae sortis* had always constituted a sizeable element. His father was a wine-cooper and a Protestant; his mother, early left a widow, was probably a Catholic convert. Challoner was born at Lewes in Sussex in 1691. In 1704 his mother became housekeeper to Lady Anastasia Holman at the Catholic Warkworth Manor in Northamptonshire, where the chaplain was John Gother. In this atmosphere the boy was brought up as a Catholic, and in 1705, shortly after Gother's death, he arrived at Douai. There he stayed, as student and professor, until 1730. He was ordained there in 1716. In 1730 Challoner journeyed to London to join the English mission as a secular priest in the metropolis, and, with only one brief return to

Douai, he remained there for forty years. He was, at first, an ordinary missioner among the poor, and then, in 1741, he was consecrated at Hammersmith to the bishopric of Debra, *in partibus infidelium*, and became coadjutor to Bishop Petre, the Vicar Apostolic who had succeeded Giffard in the London District in 1734. Shortly after Challoner's consecration, Petre retired to the family estates in Essex and the new bishop was left more or less in charge of the administration of the District, to which he succeeded formally in 1757. In the following year he secured the appointment of James Talbot, brother of the Earl of Shrewsbury, as his own coadjutor. There were around 20,000 Catholics in London, mostly in the poorer parts of the city, and the Catholic ministry lacked co-ordination and discipline: the Vicars Apostolic had no control over the Embassy Chapels at the centre and little effective voice in the appointment or conduct of the mission clergy. It was part of Challoner's great achievement to have brought some coherence to this situation. He introduced regular 'conferences' for the clergy, which were intended both to elevate their spiritual life and to bring them into some sort of ecclesiastical discipline. As with his own devotional outlook, the inspiration here came largely from the work of St Francis de Sales.

He had two other special interests. One was his polemical writing in defence of Catholicism, the first item of which, *The Unerring Authority of the Catholic Church*, appeared in 1732. He became official writer for the Chapter of the secular clergy. These works showed no originality of mind and a generally conservative representation of the faith. His devotional writings were much more enduring—*The Garden of the Soul* remained a standard and greatly loved Catholic manual until well into the twentieth century. In 1749 he revised the Douai Bible, removing a lot of the archaic Latinisms, and in 1741 he had produced *The Memoirs of Missionary Priests*, an account of the English Catholic martyrs under Elizabeth and until 1684. From this last work, and from Charles Dodd's *Church History of England*, published in 1742, English Catholic martyrology derived some of its most authoritative inspiration. Challoner's second special interest lay in education. Despite the hazards of the penal laws, he founded the school at Standon Lordship in Hertfordshire in 1749, which eventually moved to Old Hall Green and became St Edmund's College. He also founded Sedgley Park for boys and Brook Green for girls.

Challoner's own poverty, and the hardship he must have endured through insecurity and the demands of his work among the poor in London, helped him achieve his deserved reputation as the most revered English Catholic of the century. He was in most things conventional: a Jacobite by sympathy, he yet avoided political involvement and came to recognize Hanoverian legitimacy; a critic of the spirit of the Enlightenment, he was nevertheless the senior figure in a Church whose leading thinkers were influenced by it; an opponent of the regular clergy, he still managed to secure a papal ruling against their claims which left room for mutual accommodations. For this last, *Apostolicum Ministerium*, in 1753, he had worked closely with Bishop John Stonor of the Midland District and Bishop Edward Dicconson of the Northern. In 1755 he tried to prevent the appointment of a regular as Vicar Apostolic of the Western District (their informal preserve) but, having failed, he established better relations with the regulars thereafter. Challoner was a man whose great strength lay in his own devotional life, in his spiritual priorities. Early in June 1780 he left London to avoid the Gordon Riots, and returned later that month to the sorrow of apparently seeing so much of his work undone—Catholicism set back, so it seemed, by a monstrous upsurge of popular hatred and actual anti-Catholic violence. He died, at the age of eighty-nine, in January of the following year.

The Gordon Riots, as it turned out, had been something of a last gasp from an expiring organism: popular anti-Catholicism indeed survived, for more than a century, but the constitutional spirit and the political will to maintain the penal laws against professions of religious faith were decaying away. There were attempts to revive prosecutions under the laws in 1765, through the action of common informers and bounty-hunters seeking the £100 reward for procuring the prosecution of a priest under the terms of the Act of 1699. In 1767 William Payne initiated a series of prosecutions against fifteen priests and four Catholic schoolteachers. Father John Baptist Maloney, in consequence, became the last priest in England to be imprisoned under the penal laws—his sentence of life detention was commuted to exile in 1771. The other prosecutions failed, owing to the courts' insistence, under Lord Mansfield's ruling in King's Bench, on requiring absolute proof of ordination. Neither the Government nor the leaders of the State Church wanted the penal laws activated. The spirit of the times was against them: Burke later spoke of them as 'the bigotry of a free country in an enlightened age'. The Quebec Act, in 1774, gave official parliamentary recognition to the rights of the Catholic Church in Lower Canada, and the process of dismantling the penal code was just about to begin in England itself.

Neither Challoner and the Vicars Apostolic nor the Catholic clergy were involved in the first Relief Act of 1778. It was introduced by Sir George Savile after negotiations with lay Catholics in a committee headed by Lord Petre. The committee stood in the long tradition of the Appellants of 1600; they were anxious to frame an oath of loyalty to the Crown which excluded any allegiance but the most strictly spiritual to Rome. William Sheldon, a prominent member, breathed the authentic spirit of the lay-dominated Church when he declared his opposition to 'any application to the clergy in temporal matters, the English Roman Catholic Gentlemen being quite able to judge and act for themselves in these affairs'. And indeed they did. The oath of loyalty agreed by the committee denounced Stuart claims to the throne, denied that the papacy had any jurisdiction in England, and declared that no Roman authority could release Catholics from their oaths. Challoner was shown the oath only after it was agreed, and he endorsed it. The Act was passed in May 1778, and, with some amendments made by the House of Lords, went into effect. Those subscribing the new oath could now legally purchase and inherit land, and the prosecution of priests by informers, and life imprisonment, was abolished. An attempt to legislate on comparable lines for Scotland in 1779, however, elicited serious rioting in several Scottish cities. A heightened atmosphere in England was made worse by John Wesley, who in January of 1780 published a pamphlet in which he referred to the 'purple power of Rome advancing by hasty strides to overspread this once more happy land'. In the same month the Protestant Association got up by Lord George Gordon presented a petition for the repeal of the 1778 Relief Act, and rioting broke out in several parts of the capital. In the disturbances several Catholic chapels were wrecked, including the Moorfields chapel; and the Old Ship Tavern, where Challoner used to say Mass, was demolished by the mob. Newgate Gaol was burned down; Lord Petre's London house was sacked. The Protestant Archbishop of York, who had supported the Relief Act in the House of Lords, was assaulted in the streets. Two hundred and eighty-five people died in the Gordon Riots, and twenty-one were executed afterwards. But the blood-letting was not the preliminary to a new phase of anti-Catholic hostility; rather it was a sort of national purging. The gradual process of Catholic Emancipation had in reality begun.

4 The era of Emancipation and expansion

A paradoxical outcome of the movement for Catholic Emancipation—for the removal of the penal laws and for the re-entry of Catholics into Parliament itself—was an increase in Roman influence over the English Church. For although the lay Catholics who conducted the campaign went to considerable lengths in emphasizing their detachment from papal jurisdiction, it was the clergy who really gained in authority. The appeals to Rome to decide about the acceptability of the new oaths, the example of organization, and the emergence of a Catholic middle class without loyalties to the old landed families, all tended to give the clergy a new role. The way was prepared for the ultramontanes, in the mid-nineteenth century, to centralize the Church: the Vicars Apostolic, during the Emancipation struggle, had already begun to co-ordinate their actions on a national scale in order to prevent the lay Catholics from accepting a 'Gallican' understanding of English Catholicism. The lay leaders were anxious to claim a place in the professions and in the system of local influence which lay at the basis of the political system. To the Vicars Apostolic it looked as if they were quite prepared to surrender essential Catholic beliefs in the spiritual jurisdiction of the papacy in order to derive some benefit from the Protestant Constitution. No one could as yet foresee the great nineteenth-century transformation of the Constitution—the creation of the liberal modern State—and the preparedness of the lay Catholics to accept terms for entry into the existing order incompatible with papal authority sent the clergy off to Rome to get guidance and authority. The emergence of middle-class Catholics was more marked in Ireland than in England, and the Irish dimension of the issue became important. It was the first time Irish Catholicism really impinged upon the English Catholics—the Act of Union between the two countries in 1800 had brought Irish political questions to Westminster. The five million

Irish Catholics provided a mass and popular basis to the claim for Emancipation which the English Catholics had certainly lacked before. The Irish also provided a leader; and in Daniel O'Connell's various political movements the Irish middle classes found a vehicle for their entry into public life. By an Act of 1793 the franchise was extended to forty-shilling freeholder Catholics in Ireland.

In England, relief measures following the breakthrough of 1778 began to provide a practical exemption of Catholics from the severities of the old penal code. An Act of 1791 gave legal existence to registered Catholic places of worship, and Catholics were admitted to the professions. A number of successive Catholic organizations promoted the changes. The leading lay figure in this was Charles Butler, the most active member of the Catholic committee of 1782. Educated at Douai, he was ascetic and dedicated; the first Catholic barrister in England under the new dispensations. Of the ecclesiastics to emerge during the Emancipation struggle the most formidable was John Milner. Indeed, his influence endured for decades within English Catholicism. Milner was born in London in 1752, the son of a tailor, and was educated at Sedgley Park and Douai. In 1777 he was ordained and served as a mission priest in London and in Winchester. He became Vicar Apostolic of the Midland District in 1803 (and Bishop, *in partibus*, of Castabala). Until his death in 1826 he was almost constantly in the forefront of Catholic controversies. He had developed early antiquarian interests, and became a competent but not original scholar; he eschewed politics but retained a conventional belief in the compatibility of radicalism and atheism. His public disputes with Bishops Douglass and Poynter, and with Butler, over the Emancipation question, were born of his passionate conviction that Catholicism was under a grave internal threat: that the lay leaders, with the acquiescence of some of the higher clergy, were about to compromise the spiritual authority of the faith in order to secure civil liberties. Milner's divergences from the other Vicars Apostolic were heightened by his support of the Jesuits: he joined in the old dispute of the seculars and regulars, and in consequence his reputation suffered through anti-Jesuit intrigue in Rome. Even Pius VII referred to Milner as 'a firebrand'. In all truth he expressed himself unrestrainedly in controversy. Yet he achieved a very considerable lay following, especially amongst the middle-class Catholics of the Midlands. They seem to have felt some sympathy for his opposition to the lay Catholic committees in London, with their aristocratic composition; and his insistence on the priority of the spiritual over the national note in English Catholicism appealed to their sense of Catholic independence.

Milner's great rival was William Poynter, Vicar Apostolic of the London District. He, too, had been educated at Douai. Then he taught at St Edmund's College, Ware, becoming President of the College, a post he held concurrently with being coadjutor of the London District from 1803. Poynter was a supporter of the old gentry Catholicism, and an opponent of the regulars. It was not surprising, therefore, that he should have been drawn into conflict with Milner. The two were very different in temperament, also. Poynter was moderate in opinion, and diplomatic. He wanted a Catholic presence in English public life and was prepared to compromise in order to achieve a satisfactory Emancipation Act. This involved his skills to the utmost, since some of the laity were willing to make very large denials of papal power in order to declare their loyalty to the Crown and Constitution. Some were even prepared to take the existing Oath of Supremacy. Sir John Throckmorton, who was among them, published three tracts in 1790 arguing for a lay voice in the appointment of Catholic bishops. During the first decade of the nineteenth century a pamphlet entitled *Roman Catholic Principles with Regard to God and the King* was widely circulated and much discussed. It denied any papal claims to jurisdiction except over the most narrowly spiritual concerns. Milner was still denouncing it as late as 1823. Some members of the Catholic committee called themselves the 'Protesting Catholic Dissenters', a title indicative of their desire to associate Catholicism with the political and moral ethos of radical Protestant Dissent. Milner called them 'schismatical'. In 1788 they produced a 'Protestation' which denied papal temporal powers; three of the Vicars Apostolic and 240 priests signed it. But that was as far as they would go. In 1789 the Vicars Apostolic met at Hammersmith and condemned the oath proposed for inclusion in an Emancipation settlement by the Protesting Catholic Dissenters, and claimed the right of scrutiny of all similar proposals before lay assent could be given. It was a reversal, in effect, of the position adopted by Challoner over the first relief measure. A period of tension had begun between the lay leaders and the senior clergy, in the transition to clerical supremacy in the Church. Since the very start of the Catholic committee in 1782, Milner had denounced 'that system of lay interference and domination in the ecclesiastical affairs of English Catholics which has perpetuated divisions and irreligion among too many of them'. But it was in fact the clergy who were the innovators. Their claims to a decisive voice in the Emancipation debate amounted to a break with the immediate past.

Each of the organizations which promoted the Catholic claims showed an increasing tendency to fall under clerical control. The first Catholic committee of 1778 consisted of five laymen; the Cisalpine Club, formed by leading members of the committee in 1792, was the height of their influence. The Club stressed the benefits of the British Constitution and loyalty to the Crown. It was anti-papal in the sense that its members articulately eschewed 'foreign' interference both in English Catholicism and in the life of the nation generally. The Club, with its upper-class membership, was in reality the last expression of gentry management of the Church. Early in the nineteenth century it became more a social than a political body, for by then the clergy were already interfering in the movement for Emancipation. The Catholic Board, set up in 1808 as a propagandist organization to present the Catholic case, soon fell to clerical influence. All four of the Vicars Apostolic were members—although Milner was expelled from its Executive in 1813 because of his refusal to compromise over the terms of Emancipation which were then being proposed. O'Connell's Catholic Association in Ireland, and its English counterpart set up in 1823, were movements of the middle-class Catholics, a deliberate contrast to the aristocratic influences in the Church. The clergy acted as local agents, so enhancing their position still more. The Vicars Apostolic were on the committee, and all the clergy were *ipso facto* members.

In view of the lay Catholic history of division over the propriety of subscribing the Oath of Supremacy, from the Appellant controversy of 1600 to the Cisalpine Club of 1792, it was hardly surprising that the terms of Emancipation should have provoked further Catholic controversy. In the debate inside the Church, as in Parliament, in the first thirty years of the nineteenth century, it was the question of 'securities' which proved the most divisive: the checks to be placed upon Catholics as a safeguard to the Constitution should they be admitted to the legislature. The form of oath to be taken was the

centre of the difficulty. The existing parliamentary oath, which
denied the 'ecclesiastical' and 'spiritual' jurisdiction of the Pope, as
well as temporal powers, was clearly not acceptable. The Vicars
Apostolic differed among themselves about the extent to which the
new oath could still retain some disavowal of papal jurisdiction. The
next difficulty was the 'veto'—a further security giving the Crown
the right to delete the names of candidates for vacant sees. Then
there was the proposal for the *Exequatur*, the right of the Crown to
scrutinize documents arriving from Rome. Each of these securities
was found in other countries—usually Catholic countries—and in
many other places they were fruitful of controversy in the eighteenth
and nineteenth centuries, as governments sought new measures of
control over the Church, and as the Vatican sought guarantees for its
spiritual independence in the secular atmosphere of emergent
liberalism. England, in the perspective of the papacy, was a minor
example of a major difficulty. Another security proposed in these
years, however, was very much within Catholic polity—the idea of
State stipends for the Catholic clergy, a way of attaching them to the
Constitution by neutralizing their financial dependence on their
flocks. The Catholic Church upheld the principle of a relationship
between Church and State; but it was precisely because State
stipends would have forged such a relationship that the idea was
eventually dropped in England. Burdett's Emancipation Bill, in
1825, was the last legislative proposal for it, and although Wellington
would have liked to include it in his Act of 1829, all other members
of the Cabinet were opposed.

Of those securities the most divisive was the veto. In 1810 the
Catholic Board approved the principle (in rather guarded language)
in the fifth resolution of a crucial meeting at the St Alban's Tavern in
London. Of the three Vicars Apostolic present, two signed the
resolution: Poynter of London and Collingridge of the Western
District. Milner, who had before supported veto proposals, was now
passionately opposed to it. The endorsement of the fifth resolution
by a synod in London also divided the English from the Irish
agitation for Emancipation, for in Ireland the rising Catholic
movement of which O'Connell was later the leader came to reject the
veto as a sign of its separation from aristocratic domination. This
division, almost as much as Protestant opposition, and the refusal of
the Crown to violate the Coronation Oath, was responsible for

Emancipation being postponed for so long. When, in 1813, the Irish pro-Emancipationist Henry Grattan carried several parliamentary resolutions in favour of a relief measure containing a veto, the Vicars Apostolic showed their differences of view: three accepted the proposals and Milner was against. In 1814 Rome ruled in favour of the majority opinion. During the dispersal of the papal court, and Pius VII's absence in Paris, Mgr. Jean Baptiste Quarantotti delivered a judgement favourable to conceding a veto to the British Crown. The Pope, who was unhappy about Quarantotti's integrity on such issues—he had taken an oath of allegiance to Napoleon—then announced a reconsideration of the question, and the result was Cardinal Litta's statement, in 1815, endorsing a limited veto. Legislation proposed for Emancipation by Plunket in 1821 contained both a veto and the *Exequatur*, as well as the Oath of Supremacy with an explanatory declaration implying that no essential Catholic doctrines were denied. In Ireland O'Connell welcomed the plan, despite his opposition to the securities, and in England Milner was opposed. Poynter consulted Rome and went for a series of negotiated modifications. These were partially successful, and the legislation was passed in the House of Commons but defeated in the Lords by 39 votes. In 1825, when Sir Francis Burdett attempted another settlement, the Irish element supervened. The Bill was actually drawn up by O'Connell, and the English Catholics were not consulted. It contained a new oath, a veto, and *Exequatur*. The disfranchisement of the forty-shilling freeholders in Ireland, and State payments to the Catholic clergy in Ireland, were proposed in two additional 'wings' to the Bill. Poynter gave a guarded support to the plan, and Milner, again, was hostile. The Bill itself passed the Commons and was defeated in the Lords.

Popular opposition to Emancipation continued to derive from traditional prejudices about the nature of Catholicism, and from a belief that the papacy was still intent upon the subversion of the throne and Constitution. It was remarkable, however, that no significant public disturbances were got up against the various attempts at legislation—especially as these decades, suffering from the cyclical economic conditions that characterized the years after the Napoleonic Wars, were subject to a good deal of popular unrest and petty rioting. The Brunswick clubs and other organizations to prevent Catholic concessions were never very effective. Emancipation itself was the work of educated opinion: it was an example of parliamentary attitudes leading opinion in general. Many parliamentarians shared the popular prejudices about Catholicism. They also feared for the consistency of the Constitution, should men who were not of the Established Church become entitled to join what was in constitutional theory—and often in reality—its governing body. Opposition to Emancipation was because the maintenance of the union of Church and State was perceived to be the great guarantee of liberty, the centre of the liberal benefits of the British political tradition. Most of those who came to favour Emancipation shared this scheme of values: but they feared for the survival of the Constitution should it adhere to illiberal exclusions, and should the pressure from the five million Irish Catholics become too great. It was the representation of both these conditions which was the prelude to legislation in 1829. As a concession to Protestant Dissent, the Test and Corporation Acts were repealed in 1828, and this proved a useful precedent for those urging wider religious toleration. The Clare election of July 1828 in Ireland, and O'Connell's victory at the polls, precipitated the conversions of Wellington and Peel and led to the Emancipation Bill introduced to the Cabinet in January of the next year. The King at last overcame his scruples about the terms of his Coronation Oath and allowed the measure to proceed. The Emancipation Act, as passed, prescribed a new parliamentary oath which denied papal deposing powers and any 'temporal or civil jurisdiction' of the Pope in England. Catholics were also obliged to swear that they would not subvert the Establishment of the Church of England. No Catholic priest was to sit in the House of Commons. Nearly all the offices were opened to Catholics—only those of Lord Chancellor, Keeper of the Great Seal, Lord Lieutenant of Ireland, and High Commissioner of the Church of Scotland being still reserved to Protestants. Catholics could become members of corporations. No Catholic bishop was to assume a territorial title traditionally attached to the State Church. The Catholic clergy were not allowed to officiate outside their own places of worship. A clause banning religious orders from the realm—aimed at the Jesuits, whose formal reconstitution in England came in a papal decree which arrived just as the Bill was being formulated in the Cabinet—was never put into effect. There were two 'wings' to the Act: the forty-shilling freeholders in Ireland were disfranchised, and the Catholic Association in Ireland was disbanded. There was no veto or *Exequatur*. The Act passed into law in April 1829. There had been no formal consultation with Catholic opinion. Both Milner and Poynter were by then dead, and the Government acted without negotiated clauses—without the sort of procedures adopted in the legislative attempts of 1810, 1821, and 1825. All four Vicars Apostolic met in Wolverhampton and approved the new oath, and in Ireland it was welcomed by O'Connell. Many of the old penal laws remained, and even after the collected repeal measure of 1884 some still survived. But they were quite inoperable. The Act of 1829 opened public life in England to Catholics, and in May of that year, as a first-fruit, the Earl of Surrey became the first Catholic to sit in the House of Commons. In Ireland the result of the Act was to place large and decisive areas of political life in the hands of O'Connell's mass movements.

The enhanced control over English Catholic affairs secured by the clergy during the Emancipation struggle led many, in the new mood of self-confidence, to seek a return to ordinary government of the Church by canon law and territorial episcopate. The middle years of the nineteenth century also saw the growth of ideas of ecclesiastical autonomy within the State Church, and in the colonial territories the birth of institutionally self-governing churches. English Catholics, for their part, sought independence from rule by Propaganda in Rome. By the mid-century the Vicars Apostolic were becoming accustomed to periodic consultations and to joint action, but their powers were individually derived directly from the Holy See. Their agent in Rome—usually the Rector of the English College—represented their interests, and they each made regular reports to Propaganda. But these arrangements led to frequent delays and, because the agent was usually susceptible to partisan influence, to Roman misunderstanding of the real position of things in England. One advantage that it was hoped could be secured by the creation of a proper hierarchy of bishops was the ending of lay control of ecclesiastical appointments—a legacy, still strongly defended, of gentry dominance. The penal laws had inhibited clerical ownership of Church property and in consequence every Catholic chapel in England was in the hands of lay trustees. The regular orders, with their own sizeable stake in the missions, tended to support these arrangements since they perpetuated their own independence of the seculars. For the Vicars Apostolic, however, the system was very unideal: it was not only an affront to the growing sense of clericalism but it also made the deployment of manpower in the Church dependent upon the goodwill of the laity. It was, that is to say, just like the situation among the Protestants. Even before the restoration of the hierarchy in 1850 the Vicars Apostolic had made some advances in dissolving the lay committees and in taking a limited control of Church finances.

In the seventeenth and eighteenth centuries suggestions for the creation of a hierarchy had come from the secular clergy, anxious to stress their continuity with the pre-Reformation Church and willing to make some accommodation with the political establishment as the price to pay. The nineteenth-century restoration of the hierarchy was quite different. Early advocates, it is true, urged the cause because they wanted more control of the Church by the lower clergy, and because of their adhesion to an 'Old Catholic' sense that favoured domestic government rather than rule by a Roman Congregation. Yet the movement for a hierarchy was captured and then transformed by the ultramontanes, and when it came the new system was to be the means whereby the English Church was, for a century, transformed by the 'Roman spirit'. That extraordinary achievement was largely the work of Cardinal Wiseman. But the exponents of a hierarchy had also to encounter another traditional obstacle—the religious orders.

The first half of the nineteenth century was as marked by antipathy between the seculars and the regulars as preceding centuries has been. Anti-Jesuit feeling remained strong, and was reflected in the delations to Rome of the writings of Father Peter Gandolphy made by Bishop Poynter after 1816. Gandolphy was a Stonyhurst priest whose views on the sacraments were thought by the Vicars Apostolic (Milner alone dissenting) to be unorthodox. With the application to England in 1829 of the bull *Sollicitudo Omnium Ecclesiarum* of 1814, which had restored the Society of Jesus throughout the world, fear of Jesuit influence increased. But the most difficult and disruptive dispute of these years was between the Benedictines and Bishop Baines of the Western District. Peter Augustine Baines was himself a Benedictine, professed at Ampleforth in 1804. In 1817 he was sent to serve on the mission at Bath, and in 1823 he became coadjutor to Bishop Collingridge. In this office he at once began to consider the problem of providing a seminary for the West: the training of the clergy, as for most bishops, being his major priority. His proposal that Downside monastery be turned into a seminary was resisted by the monks and by the English Benedictine Congregation, and a protracted dispute, with appeals to Rome from both parties, went on for some years. In 1829 Baines succeeded Collingridge as Vicar Apostolic, and proceeded to withdraw faculties from the Downside monks. But he did not win, and instead founded a seminary at Prior Park in Bath. Relations between the Vicars Apostolic and the regulars were worsened in 1838 when Rome issued two decrees which gave new privileges to the regular clergy operating in the English mission and allowed them to open chapels without the permission of the bishops. In 1840 the secular clergy petitioned Rome, requesting that in future no regulars should be appointed as Vicars Apostolic. There was a widespread impression among the clergy that the regulars fostered an anti-episcopal spirit. Old claims still lay at the basis of some of the regulars' attitudes. The Benedictines petitioned Gregory XVI against the immediate restoration of an English hierarchy, and urged the eventual return to themselves of the dioceses they had controlled before the Reformation. 'We have carefully kept up the canonical Election of those Cathedral Priors,' they wrote to the Pope, 'looking forward to the ultimate restoration of our ancient Hierarchy, when they would return to their canonical rights and privileges.' Mutual suspicions and practical problems of ecclesiastical demarcation continued until 1881, when the papal Constitution *Romanos Pontifices* upheld the claims of the seculars by ruling that the missions conducted by the regulars were on the same basis as others: their chapels and schools were under episcopal control. The bishops were also declared able to apportion the regulars' missions territorially and to appoint priests to new missions created as a result. In the hundred years after the restoration of the hierarchy in 1850, all but seven of the bishops were appointed from among the seculars.

The movement for the re-establishment of a hierarchy was therefore in part inspired by the seculars' hope of gaining full control over the English Church; it also derived from the ultramontanes' desire to enhance Roman influence. When the old Catholic committee had urged a hierarchy in 1782 it had been concerned with lay rights in the patronage and trusts of the missions: the laymen who had dominated its proceedings sought to domesticate the government of the Church, to bring it back to England and away from the direct authority of Propaganda. In 1837 the 'Old Catholic' clergy of the Northern District petitioned Propaganda for a voice in the election of bishops and for the creation of normal parochial districts under canon law. It was this sort of sentiment—probably quite widespread in the English Church—which persuaded the Vicars Apostolic of the need to take over the movement for a hierarchy before it turned into a species of 'Gallicanism'. They sought, that is to say, to counter the influence of Dr Daniel Rock, Father Mark Tierney, and the Adelphi Club: the clergy association aimed at the provision of a hierarchy responsive to control by the lower clergy and the laity.

In 1837 the Vicars Apostolic approached Gregory XVI. He was willing to increase the number of Vicariates for reasons of administrative efficiency but, fearing Crown interference with ecclesiastical appointments under a properly constituted hierarchy, desired to go no further for the time being. Thus in 1840 the Eastern, Central, Welsh, and Lancastrian Districts were created: the number of the Vicariates was doubled. The English bishops, however, still sought a full restoration, because of the need to bring Roman discipline and influence to bear through a centralizing of the missions, and some because they wanted additional armour against the regulars. In 1847 Pius IX was persuaded of the case, and an actual scheme was drawn up. This was shown to Lord Minto, who was in Rome at the time as special envoy of the British Government in Italy, and his lack of opposition encouraged the papacy to proceed. The Catholic Emancipation Act of 1829 forbade Catholic prelates to adopt territorial ecclesiastical titles employed by State Church functionaries in England, and although the Catholics were reluctant to give up the ancient titles, it was politic to name the dioceses to be created after other cities. Some delays in implementing the scheme resulted from the settlement of this matter, as they did from arriving at the names of the first bishops. Then the Revolution broke out in Rome, and in November 1848 the Pope fled to Gaeta. The plans for the English hierarchy, together with most other papal business, lapsed, and it was not until Pius IX's return to Rome, in April 1850, that the scheme was resumed. The Brief restoring the hierarchy in England was dated 29 September, and on 7 October Nicholas

Wiseman, now raised as a cardinal to head the hierarchy, issued his Pastoral Letter out of the Flaminian Gate. 'Catholic England has been restored to its orbit in the ecclesiastical firmament, from which its light had long vanished,' he declared, 'and begins anew its course of regularly adjusted action round the centre of unity, the source of jurisdiction, of light and of vigour.' And that was what it was all about: the reception of the 'Roman spirit', the authority of papal monarchy, the devotional style of triumphalist Italian Catholicism.

As Wiseman was making his slow return to England the worst anti-Catholic uproar since the Gordon Riots of 1780 broke out. It was *The Times* which was largely to blame. A number of papers had reported the setting-up of the hierarchy, with no evident effect upon public opinion. The Government had known of the proposals through Lord Minto. But *The Times* fulminated against Wiseman and Rome in all the most characteristic 'No Popery' language it could command: 'The Pope and his advisers have mistaken our complete tolerance for indifference to their designs; they have mistaken the renovated zeal of the Church in this country for a return towards Romish bondage.' Already, therefore, in *The Times* assault lay the association of High Church tendencies in the Church of England, released in a radical form through the Oxford Movement, with adhesion to Rome. The conversions of Newman and other Anglicans to Catholicism in the preceding decade were now recalled with renewed bitterness. The Prime Minister, Lord John Russell, published his 'Letter to the Bishop of Durham' in November. He denounced the 'assumption of power' and the 'pretension to supremacy over the realm of England' in the papal Brief and in Wiseman's Pastoral, and again linked the buoyancy of Catholicism with the 'renegades' of the National Church. The Archbishop of Canterbury called the Catholic priesthood 'insinuating', and the Bishop of London said they were 'emissaries of darkness'. It was not a good start for Wiseman. Pius IX, unable to imagine why the public mind was so disturbed about a matter for so long in preparation, remarked of the English: 'You are a very strange people. You seem to me to understand nothing thoroughly but commerce.'

Wiseman arrived in London to face several threats to his life. He set down his justification of the hierarchy at once, and published it as a tract entitled *An Appeal to the Reason and Good Feeling of the*

English People. In December 1850 he delivered a series of lectures at St George's Cathedral in Southwark which also presented the case for the hierarchy. In both, he denied that any papal pretensions existed over the temporal affairs of the kingdom—which was plainly the truth—and explained the hierarchy as a simple matter of ecclesiastical autonomy, like that claimed by the English Dissenters. In 1851 the Government replied with the Ecclesiastical Titles Act, which reinforced the existing prohibition of Catholics' assuming territorial titles held by the clergy of the Church of England. But Wiseman's temperate words, in such contrast to the florid and triumphalist rhetoric of the Flaminian Gate Pastoral, had their effect. The public sensation passed. Some public men like Gladstone were shocked by the government legislation, believing it late in the day to pass laws against the free exercise of religion. Popular 'No Popery' remained latent in society, however, and in educated circles, too, it could still summon up echoes from the past when needed: it was Gladstone, also, who was to denounce the Vatican Council as a reassertion of papal temporal claims. The period between 1850 and Gladstone's controversy over the Vatican Decrees in 1874, in fact, was one marked by a vigorous and literate anti-Catholicism in English public life, with periodic petty rioting got up by popular Protestant speakers. But, although this was scarcely evident to the Catholics of the time, the real threat to the Catholics had already passed away: they had successfully claimed their place within the emergent religious pluralism of nineteenth-century English liberalism.

The restored hierarchy of 1850 was greeted with mixed responses among the 'Old Catholics' and the remnants of the Catholic gentry class. Many discerned the truth: that it was the symbol of Roman control over their Church, the final sign of the eclipse of their long hegemony. The ultramontane party were delighted, and so were most of the new band of converts from Anglicanism. The consequences of the hierarchy were to be detected in heightened morale and in a quiet extension of the influence of the clergy over the laity, rather than in any dramatic change in the way the Church in England operated. Centralization under the scheme was limited. Although Wiseman sometimes behaved as if he had power over the other bishops—which was what the public and the press always assumed he had—his rights were not extensive. He could preside at national synods and had appellate jurisdiction, but each of the bishops was independently responsible to Rome, and they carefully preserved their rights. The hierarchy, in consequence, inaugurated a new period of tension in the Church, as Wiseman and the bishops differed over a series of important issues in which he expected his authority to be respected. As Archbishop of Westminster, however, his authority scarcely extended beyond his own metropolitan see. The institutional effects of the hierarchy were also limited, because a full restoration of autonomy had not in fact occurred. Propaganda continued to supervise English affairs, and it was not until Pius X's *Sapienti Consilio* in 1908 that normal relations with Rome were effected; it was not until 1918 that canon law was applied in England and ordinary parishes came into existence. Diocesan synods began to be held after 1853 and thereafter met every few years, and there were periodic provincial synods of all the bishops, who also met together annually in Low Week to discuss common matters and to co-ordinate relations with Rome. The synods began to produce consolidated diocesan administration, with deanery conferences carrying out the decisions. The contemporaneous massive pro-grammes of church and school building, required by the Irish immigration, and the consequent enormous increase of the Catholic population, also tended to stimulate diocesan administrative machin-ery and control. The last remnants of lay involvement in ecclesiasti-cal administration were swept away in the floods of diocesan fund-raising. It was a time of extraordinary energy and quite outstanding achievement. Even had there been no restoration of the hierarchy in 1850, sheer force of circumstance would doubtless have forced the rapid evolution of some sort of Catholic ecclesiastical *apparat*. But in giving structure to the confidence and enthusiasm which ran through the Church of the mid-nineteenth century, the advent of the new system was a timely assistance.

The atmosphere of buoyancy in the Church in some measure derived from increased numbers. It came also from the physical evidence of revival—of the churches, convents, schools and Catholic institutional buildings which were appearing everywhere as a testimony to the emergence, as it seemed to contemporaries, from the catacombs of the penal era. As Newman declared in his most famous sermon, preached at the First Provincial Synod of Westminster: 'It is the coming in of a second Spring; it is a restoration in the moral world.' Catholic expansion was actually a part of a more general British phenomenon of the nineteenth century: all the Churches were in a confident mood, as they battled against the infidelity of the slums, sought to bring education to the children of the poor, and associated the moral seriousness of the age with Christian values. That Catholicism was able to take part in the new religious vitality was a remarkable testimony to its responsiveness to the opportunities presented by the atmosphere of liberal toleration; it became a part of the new religious pluralism of public life and can, to that extent, be described as having entered into a 'denominational' role. That role was never frankly acknowledged, however, nor was it ever complete: the Catholic triumphalism of the ultramontane spirit which came to dominate the leadership of the Church under Wiseman, Manning, and Vaughan, and the continued popular hostility to the 'foreign' character of the Catholic Church, inhibited the appearance of a real denominational self-consciousness. At the popular level, too, the Catholics lacked that sense of integration with a pattern of diversity which is inseparable from denominationalism. Many of the parishes in the cities were overwhelmingly Irish in composition, and it was not until the second or even third generation that their outlook—by then anyway tempered through the 'leakage' from the faith of many of their co-religionists—embraced the conception of the Church as one among others. The prohibition of mixed marriages assisted the exclusivity of Catholicism.

A clear indication of the expansion of the Church was the anti-Catholic popular reaction it elicited. There were 'No Popery' riots at Birkenhead in 1850, and in 1852, in the notorious Stockport riots, two Catholic chapels were sacked by a Protestant mob. Of the popular orators, Alessandro Gavazzi and William Murphy—the one an ex-monk from Naples, and the other an Irish militant—were the ones whose addresses most frequently inspired disturbances. After one of Murphy's harangues in 1868 a hundred houses and two Catholic churches were destroyed by the crowd who heard his denunciations of Rome. But these were surface phenomena; beneath lay a solid foundation of Catholic advance. In 1850 there were 587 Catholic churches in England and Wales and 788 clergy; in 1900 there were 1,529 churches and 2,812 clergy. The religious census of 1851 yielded a Catholic population of 252,783—something of an underestimate, since there were already in that year 519,959 persons in the country who were of Irish birth, a very high proportion of whom must have been Catholics. The Irish immigration had also radically changed the distribution pattern of Catholicism in England. It had enormously reinforced the existing trend to urbanization of the members, evident since the mid-eighteenth century, and provided, for the first time, a large working-class membership.

Yet to most observers it was the converts from Anglicanism who seemed to show the new vitality of the Church. This was mistaken: most of the converts were repelled by the erastianism of the English State Church rather than attracted by that they took to be Catholicism. Few had much knowledge of the institution they joined, and very few were actually converted through the agency of the Catholic clergy. As Luigi Gentili reported to Rome in 1847, 'nearly all came after reading the Fathers or our books; it was not because of our efforts'. Some of the most famous were attracted through the 'medievalism' of nineteenth-century taste. Kenelm Digby, Ambrose Phillipps de Lisle, and George Spencer sought to find in Catholicism the authentic embodiment of a medieval 'age of faith'. Some liked the triumphalist note of the Church as understood by Wiseman. Thus Manning, W. G. Ward, and Faber were more devoted to Roman practices than the English Catholics they joined. Still others, like Newman or Pugin, found the quiet atmosphere of traditional English Catholicism more satisfactory. The Oxford Movement swept in the intellectuals and the disillusioned Anglican clergy, with Newman's conversion in 1845 and Manning's in 1851 as high-water marks. The converts, however, were statistically a negligible part of the Catholic expansion, most of which resulted from the Irish presence. Their importance, externally speaking, lay in their impact on their contemporaries. The Protestants they left behind were made aware that Catholicism was a force to be reckoned with, and the Catholics exaggerated the extent to which they were precursors of a flood to come. Wiseman, in Rome as Rector of the English College in the early days of the Oxford Movement, was convinced that the Church of England was near to collapse, and it was his conveyance of this vision to the Roman authorities which made them, in turn, impatient with the English Catholics for not grasping the opportunities seemingly to hand. The mutual antipathies of the Old Catholics and the converts were, for half a century or more, a feature of English Catholicism. The Old Catholics, anyway on the defensive against the Romanizing policies of the ultramontanes, could not bring themselves to believe in the sincerity of the converts. The converts were shocked by the intellectual crudity, as it seemed to them, of the Catholics they joined. 'When a Catholic meets a Protestant in controversy,' W. G. Ward said to Jowett in 1858, 'it is like a barbarian meeting a civilized man.' It was not surprising in these circumstances that Phillipps de Lisle's attempt in the 'Association for the Promotion of the Unity of Christendom', founded in 1857, to bring about a reunion of Anglicanism and Catholicism, should have foundered: in 1864 Rome instructed the faithful to keep out of it.

The Irish immigrants created the numbers of the Church of the nineteenth century and also its financial problems, as the attempt to keep up with church and school building ran into the obvious difficulty that the Irish were also the poorest section of society. During the famine years of the 1840s immigration dramatically increased. Often there were problems with the sedate English Catholics among whom they settled. The Anglican converts, too, had not quite believed that the Church of the Fathers would have a Kerry accent. In practice real clashes were rare: the Irish tended to settle in urban concentrations which had not before had a Catholic population, and where there was contact with the natives a practical segregation often occurred. In Birmingham, for example, the Irish worshipped at St Chad's Cathedral and the English attended St Peter's Church. Despite their poverty, the Irish were actually a beneficial influence in the Church. Their sheer numbers galvanized the clergy into working-class missions and obliged English Catholicism to become a mass organization with a multi-class basis; their financial contributions were veritable widow's mites: the poor gave up what they could ill afford in honour of their religion, and the whole Church was ennobled by the experience. In some places the Irish population became quite large. In 1881 the Irish constituted 12.8 per cent of the population of Liverpool, 7.5 per cent of Manchester, and 3.3 per cent of London. Most came from rural areas in Ireland, and it was the Catholic Church in England which helped them keep their sense of personal identity and dignity in the appalling conditions of the slum existence to which they had been translated. With acculturation, the Irish picked up English religious habits: many gave up going to Mass—'leakage' from the faith was the result. But the prohibition of mixed marriages, which helped retain a sense of Catholic identity, must also have kept many in the faith who would otherwise have lapsed, and it also accounted for the absorption of some Protestants.

An indication of the revitalizing of the Church was the expansion of the religious orders. In addition to the Benedictines and the Jesuits, the Dominicans were re-established in 1850 and the Franciscans in the same year. The Cistercians had returned in 1837 when Ambrose Phillipps de Lisle had founded Mount St Bernard's. Modifications to the rules of enclosure in the early nineteenth century enabled nuns to undertake educational work, and this led to a multiplication of orders of women in England. The most notable advances here, perhaps, were the Dominican foundations of Mother Margaret Hallahan at Coventry in 1845 and at Stone in 1853. The introduction of new missionary orders from Italy was part of the ultramontane influence generally fostered by Wiseman and his circle. In them something like a Catholic equivalent of Protestant Revivalism became apparent—there were popular and emotional orations, retreats, outdoor meetings, and, above all, the encouragement of the new devotional practices of Italy. The Rosminians arrived with Fr. Luigi Gentili in 1835. The Passionists came with Blessed Dominic Barberi in 1841, the Redemptorists were introduced by Bishop Baines in 1843, and in 1847 Newman founded the Oratorians in Birmingham. The second English house of the Oratorians was set up in London by Faber in 1849. In 1887 the Salesians began work in Battersea, at the suggestion of St John Bosco. The two leading Italian missioners, Gentili and Barberi, became the standard-bearers of the new orders and had a lasting impact on the style of English Catholicism. They were the most decisive force for the new devotional outlook of popular Catholicism, and helped to a stamp Catholic worship—through adoration of the Sacred Heart, the use of the rosary, reverence for the Immaculate Conception, the Forty Hours Devotion—with features which subsequent generations came to regard as the very substance of Catholicism itself. Father Luigi Gentili, the earliest missioner for the Institute of Charity, had first worked in teaching the boys at the Prior Park school, and it was there that he encountered Old Catholic opposition to the new devotions. Half the boys were withdrawn from the school by scandalized parents more accustomed to the 'Garden of the Soul' styles of English worship. After leaving the school in 1837, Gentili became an itinerant missioner, and his real work began among the working classes of the industrial cities. He died of fever in 1848 on a visit to Dublin, after a last exhausting four years in which he had led fifty-one missions and converted over three thousand people. Blessed Dominic Barberi, the Passionist, was the priest who admitted Newman to the Church. After arrival in England in 1841 he worked as a missioner from the houses of the order at Aston Hall and Stone in Staffordshire. There were many retreats and missions throughout the Midland counties. He died suddenly in 1849 and when, forty years later, his coffin was reopened, his body was found to have been preserved incorrupt. The great English advocate of the new devotions was Faber. Born in 1814, the son of an Anglican parson, Frederick William Faber was educated at Shrewsbury and Harrow, and at Oxford, and himself became a priest of the Church of England in 1843. After a visit to Rome, where he was impressed by the shrine of St Philip Neri in the Chiesa Nova, and where he met the Pope, he converted his rural parish of Elton into a sort of monastic community. Then, following Newman, he passed into the Catholic Church in 1845 and set up a Catholic community, first in Birmingham and then at Cotton Hall. It merged, in 1848, with Newman's Oratorians. After some differences within the order, however, Faber established a separate house in London which shortly became the great English centre of Italianate worship. In 1852 the Oratory moved to splendid new buildings at Brompton. Faber was best known, and is known to this day, for his hymns and devotional writings—especially the book *All for Jesus*, published in 1853. It was hugely popular with Catholics in his own day and greatly fostered devotions to the Virgin. Faber died in 1863.

Opposition to the new devotional styles came from those traditional English Catholics who correctly discerned that they were an external and popularized sign of a great shift of emphasis within the Church—the remoulding of English Catholicism according to the vision of the ultramontanes. Because this was the age of church building and decoration, a lot of the controversy became centred on architectural styles as well as devotional practices, and this was heightened because the Church acquired one convert of great architectural genius. Augustus Welby Pugin, born in 1812, was brought up as an Anglican and became a Catholic quite suddenly, in 1835, apparently without external influence—he had never met a Catholic priest. Trained already by his father as a draughtsman and architect, he applied himself with incredible labour to the building of Gothic churches. Pugin was a man of strongly held beliefs about style and taste, and his ideological attachment of 'authentic' Catholicism to Gothic stood in sharp and instantly divisive contrast to the preference of the ultramontanes for Italian neo-classical and baroque styles. He also supported the use of Gregorian chant in services; it became, indeed, a feature of 'English worship', as did Gothic vestments and rood-screens in churches. So sensitive were the feelings of both sides that in 1839 Propaganda actually stepped in to attempt a prohibition of Gothic vestments (and to enforce the use of the Roman chasuble instead). Pugin and the Old Catholics who identified with him regarded all Roman uses as anathema. Ancient conflicts were resuscitated around local disputes over church hangings and devotional literature. In 1847 Pugin visited Italy and was appalled by the Sistine Chapel and by St Peter's: both monuments to wrong styles. His book *Contrasts*, published in 1836, had been a moral treatise: observing bad social and religious values attached to modern neo-classicism, and Catholic virtue expressed in the Gothicism of the past. 'Before true taste and Christian feelings can be revived,' he wrote in 1843, 'all the present and popular ideas on the subject must be utterly changed.' The dogmatism of the ultramontanes with their Italian ideals of the Church, therefore, met a comparable dogmatism in the champions of 'English' Catholicism. It was not surprising that both locally and nationally the Church of the mid-century was marked by conflicts. What is often overlooked, however, is that these were by-products of vitality—the evidences of an expansive and confident mood in a body which, barely three-quarters of a century before, had scarcely been allowed by law or opinion to build any churches at all.

The public emergence of the Church was most visible in the work of education, for this brought the bishops into contact with the Government, through claims to a share in the parliamentary funds made available to the denominations for subsidies to their schools. A very large part of the resources of the Catholic Church in modern England has been allocated to the provision of schools and other institutions of learning, and the foundations were laid soon after the

Emancipation Act. Catholics have regarded it as essential to the preservation of the faith of their children that the acquisition of knowledge should be in an atmosphere of religious conviction and with a distinct Christian content. Since almost all the available popular education until the Education Act of 1870 was conducted by the State Church in England, Catholic denominational schools alone seemed able to satisfy the premises of the bishops. As liberal theology developed inside the Protestant Church, furthermore—epitomized in the publication of *Essays and Reviews* in 1860—Catholics were more than ever convinced of the need for separate education for their children. The education question also had the effect of consolidating clerical influence in the Church: the bishops centralized policy in order to co-ordinate relations with the Government. Those relations began when applications were made by Catholics for a share in the funds made available by Parliament in 1839 to the Committee for Education of the Privy Council. The bishops were initially divided about the propriety and safety of applying for grants at all—schools in receipt of grants-in-aid had to accept inspection by the State, and this, it was feared (not unreasonably), could well lead to a measure of State control.

The Catholic bishops were all concerned with education, but the one who most specialized in the question was William Bernard Ullathorne, Bishop of Birmingham and eventually titular Archbishop of Cabasa. His family was descended from St Thomas More and was very conscious of its Old Catholic pedigree. Ullathorne's father was a Yorkshire draper, and all his life the Bishop retained a rough regional accent which emphasized his main characteristic—his Englishness. Born in 1806, he was educated at a village school and then, after a short time in the family business, went to sea. There is a vivid account in his autobiography, *From Cabin-Boy to Archbishop*, of the growth of his religious vocation aboard a brig in the Baltic. In 1823 he entered the school at Downside and in 1824 became a Benedictine postulant. He was ordained to the priesthood in 1831 and in 1833 arrived in Australia as Vicar-General. There he became involved in penal reform and acquired that sense of the importance of social issues which he deployed over education questions in England after his return in 1840. In 1846 he became Vicar Apostolic of the Western District, and in 1848 he was in Rome gaining further valuable administrative experience as agent of the English bishops during the hierarchy discussions. In the new ecclesiastical arrangements of 1850 he became first Bishop of Birmingham. A Tory in politics and an anti-ultramontane by background, he nevertheless became a moderate and central figure in the hierarchy, trusted both by Wiseman's and Manning's circles in London and by the 'Old Catholics' of the provinces. In 1857 he published a lengthy tract on the education question which pointed to the hazards involved in accepting government grants, and this led to differences of view with Wiseman. The split continued. In 1870 Manning accepted the Education Act while Ullathorne was opposed to it.

Catholics first received grants for their parochial schools in 1847. One of the consequences was the setting-up of a body under the control of the bishops to treat with the Government—the Catholic Poor School Committee. In 1869, to further the building of schools and to enhance co-ordination, the bishops agreed that an Education Council should be appointed in each diocese, charged also with the return of statistics to the Poor School Committee in London. The system worked extremely effectively, and the impressive multiplication of Catholic educational facilities for the working classes was the result. By the end of the century there were nearly seven hundred Catholic elementary schools. A careful watch continued to be kept on legislation, to protect Catholic interests and to seek parity with the other denominational schools and to monitor the terms upon which State subsidies could be received. The Education Act of 1897 followed declarations of principle made by the bishops, and the abolition of the rating of voluntary (denominational) schools included in its clauses was regarded by them as a great achievement. The 1902 Act, similarly, was helpful to the Catholics. In these campaigns, in which Cardinal Vaughan exerted himself so tirelessly, Catholics and Anglicans worked on the same side against the Liberal Party and the Nonconformists. This affinity with the State Church on a major question of policy was a key factor in preventing the Catholics from acquiring a 'denominational' self-identity, for it occurred just at a time when consciousness of their place in the religious pluralism of England might otherwise have placed the Catholics on the side of Dissent.

Secondary education in the nineteenth century had got off to an earlier start, with the return to England of the exiles from the Napoleonic Wars. Together with the Jesuit College of Stonyhurst in

Lancashire (1794), the remants of Douai at St Edmund's, Ware, and Ushaw (resettled in 1793 and 1808 respectively), and the older surviving schools at Sedgley Park and Oscott, Catholic education for the sons of the gentry was well provided. At Stonyhurst, Ushaw, Oscott, and St Edmund's, boys could also proceed to vocational training for the priesthood, thus preserving in England that curious feature of the old exile colleges—the education of lay and clerical students side by side. It was to be a matter of frequent complaint by the bishops in the nineteenth century, and attempts at the creation of a Catholic university were in some measure intended to provide an alternative. Schools for the Catholic middle class were a feature of the general expansion of Catholic education during the century—institutions like Ullathorne's refoundation of Cotton College in 1873, and Vaughan's St Bede's in 1875. There were also night schools and commercial academies. The religious orders took an especially strong lead in the secondary schools, particularly in schools for girls. By the mid-century there were over fifty religious orders of women engaged in educational work. It was the Ursulines and the Sisters of Charity who took the lead in this.

Higher education was a permanent problem for the Catholics. Advanced studies were pursued at Stonyhurst and Oscott, and these colleges, together with Prior Park, Downside, and St Edmund's, affiliated to London University after its foundation in 1835 and rearranged their courses to coincide with the degree course. In this way Catholics could secure the degrees of the secular London University without having to reside in the Anglican-dominated atmospheres of Oxford and Cambridge. The new wave of converts in the mid-century, however, remained attached to the educational styles that had nurtured them, and hence the idea of a Catholic hall or college at Oxford. Both Wiseman and Ullathorne were originally attracted to this sort of scheme, as a way of encouraging a Catholic presence in the world of learning—as well as regularizing the position of the Catholics who were anyway resorting to the ancient universities. In 1864 and in 1866 plans for an Oxford college were made and abandoned. There were suspicions among the bishops about Newman's influence, for it was he who was to head the venture. In 1867 Propaganda ruled decisively against 'mixed' higher education, and although there was no formal prohibition of the attendance of Catholics at Oxford and Cambridge, parents whose sons went there were declared to be guilty of exposing them to religious and moral hazard. In 1873 the Fourth Provincial Synod of Westminster decided to emulate the Irish example—and fulfil the policy long recommended by Propaganda—of establishing a Catholic university in England. The result was the University College at Kensington, opened in 1875. But it was not successful. Mgr. Thomas Capel, Manning's choice as Rector, displayed some administrative incompetence and was obliged to resign in 1878; the religious orders and Newman failed to give support; the bishops seemed more concerned with providing professional qualifications than with learning as such; and, most decisive, the drift to the ancient universities, encouraged by the reforms of the 1850s which opened their degrees to non-Anglicans, continued. The Kensington venture came to an end in 1882. In 1895 the hierarchy abandoned its policy of exclusion and instead set up a board to arrange an orderly entry of Catholics to Oxford and Cambridge. Resident chaplains for both universities were sanctioned by Propaganda in the following year. Pressure from the laity had proved irresistible. Catholic halls of residence were established at Oxford and Cambridge.

There were two other questions which brought the bishops into contact with the Government in the nineteenth century. One was the provision of Catholic chaplains in the armed services and in workhouses and prisons—a crucial pastoral issue in view of the increasing Irish element in all of these. The Bishop of Southwark, Thomas Grant, himself the son of an army sergeant, acted for the hierarchy over chaplaincies, and in 1854, during the Crimean War, he succeeded in getting government support for the sending of Catholic nuns to serve as nurses. In 1858 he helped to persuade the Government to appoint a permanent body of Catholic military chaplains. By an Act of 1862 Catholic children could be removed from workhouses and placed in Catholic institutions at the expense of the local poor rate; in 1863 legislation provided salaried Catholic chaplains in prisons. The effects of the Emancipation Act were working through the system. But in the second question which brought the bishops into contact with the State there was a less obviously clear result. This was the question of Charitable Trusts —hugely important since existing law still declared that money and property left by testators for Catholic purposes could be confiscated on the grounds that superstitious uses were served. Legislation in 1853 which set up the Charity Commission was regarded with suspicion by the bishops, who declined to co-operate with it. They feared that, because of the state of the law, registration of their charitable trusts might lay them open to State interference and perhaps even the seizure of the properties. Propaganda, appealed to for guidance in what could potentially develop into a fearful clash of the Catholic Church and the State, ruled in 1854 that each bishop was free to act as he thought appropriate. The matter was complicated by internal strife. Wiseman's tendency to conduct affairs as if the other bishops were there for consultative purposes only, added to the problem of arriving at a single view. A test case in 1861, furthermore, decided that Masses for the dead were indeed still 'superstitious uses' in English law and that no money left for such purposes could be protected by the courts. In 1862 Propaganda ruled again, this time in support of Wiseman's belief that Catholic charities ought not to register with the State. But the issue was not brought to further test, and law reforms in the later years of the century, while not actually solving the problem, did make legal action against Catholic trusts extremely unlikely.

Catholic involvement in politics, as a further legacy of Emancipation, was not particularly distinctive in the nineteenth century. The agitation for the end of the penal laws has associated the Catholic lay leaders with liberal groups and attitudes, but this did not, except in Ireland, endure as a continuing tradition beyond Emancipation itself. Apart from fringe interest in the controversy over church rates, the Catholics kept clear of the great nineteenth-century development of Dissenting Liberal politics, partly because its educational secularism was so distasteful to them. The Ecclesiastical Titles Act in 1851 divorced the Catholic bishops from the Whig Party for a decade and a half, and the only important Catholic lay figure of militantly liberal politics of these years was Frederick Lucas, founder in 1840 of the *Tablet*, who died in 1855. The Church was not even drawn into Irish politics. This was extraordinary, in view of the huge Irish membership of English Catholic parishes. The reason lay in the nature of the leadership. Unlike the experience of America and Australia, where Irish prelates dominated distinctly Irish churches, the bishops in England remained mostly English. They were more frightened at the spread of Fenianism among the poor Irish of the industrial cities than they were concerned about Irish reforms.

Manning was perhaps the exception here, and he used his influence with Gladstone—an influence which fluctuated markedly over the years—to represent Irish Catholic views on Irish legislation. The rise of Gladstonianism, in fact, embraced most of local urban Catholicism, and by the 1870s the Irish of the cities were becoming fairly solidly Liberal in sympathy. The sign of this came with T. P. O'Connor (elected as a Liverpool MP in 1880), whose United Irish League of Great Britain organized the Irish Catholic vote and attached it to the Home Rule cause in 1885. The bishops did not align themselves politically until the rise of the education question obliged a practical support for the Conservatives as the party of denominational schools. Even then, they avoided partisan declarations. With the exception, again, of Manning, and of Edward Bagshawe, Bishop of Nottingham, the Catholic leadership was not noticeably taken up with the politics of social reform, as the Anglican leadership increasingly was in the last decades of the century. The publication of Leo XIII's *Rerum Novarum* in 1891, with its encouragement of a more 'social' Catholicism, made only a slight impact among the English Catholics. The bishops were preoccupied with educational, charitable, temperance, and 'rescue' work among the working classes: they did not regard political and collectivized solutions as the appropriate ones for ecclesiastical leaders to promote. Christian Socialism developed more slowly within English Catholicism than among the Protestants, and the Catholic Socialist Society was not founded until 1906. The bishops emphasized pastoral, not political, work as the salvation of the poor.

5 Leaders and thinkers

Victorian Catholicism benefited from some remarkable leaders. In its ultramontane ecclesiastical statesmen, Wiseman, Manning, and Vaughan, and in its scholars and thinkers, Newman, Ward, and Acton, it had persons of eminence who were capable of speaking to the other great men of their generation. These were figures who led the Catholics into the arena of public life; whose contributions were, in different ways, to place a permanent stamp on modern Catholicism in England.

Nicholas Wiseman's career was divided into Roman and English phases. He was born at Seville in 1802, the son of a merchant whose family came from Ireland. After the father's death, which occurred when Wiseman was still young, the family returned to Waterford, and the boy was educated there until, in 1810, he was sent to Ushaw. In 1818 he departed for Rome as one of the first group of seminarists chosen to study at the reopened English College, and he remained there for the ensuing twenty-two years. In 1825 he was raised to the priesthood, and in 1828 he was made Rector of the College. He also became, as was usual, agent of the English Vicars Apostolic and began to take an interest in the affairs of the Church in England. By upbringing and residence, he had little actual knowledge of the English Catholic Church, and ultramontane sympathies therefore came easily to one who had virtually no acquaintance with the peculiar atmosphere of Old Catholic life. In 1835, on a visit to England, he delivered a series of public lectures which was the first presentation, intended for Protestant audiences, of Catholic doctrine, and he achieved a good deal of sympathetic attention. During his stay he also took part in the foundation of the *Dublin Review*, to which, during the next twenty years, he contributed some seventy articles: it was from these that he first became known to the Catholic public in England. In 1840 Wiseman returned to England again—this time as coadjutor to Bishop Walsh in the Central

District. His first contribution to the development of the Church in England was to gather together at Oscott, in Birmingham, some of the most distinguished of the Anglican converts whom the tides of the Oxford Movement had deposited upon the Catholic strand. His experience of Roman administration, and his friendship with the officials of Propaganda, made Wiseman a useful person to represent English affairs, and in 1847 he was in Rome again over the hierarchy question; he was also charged by the Holy See with exploring the possibility of diplomatic relations with England.

Despite his comparative youth and inexperience of England, it was therefore not surprising that in 1850 the papacy named him as head of the restored hierarchy and dignified him with a cardinal's hat. It was Wiseman's genius that turned the new ecclesiastical structure into the means by which ultramontane influence was spread in England. This was to lead to some unhappy friction with the Old Catholics and especially with George Errington, his coadjutor after 1855 and a contemporary of Wiseman's at Ushaw and the English College. Errington embodied the Old Catholic spirit, and he regarded Wiseman's autocratic grandeur as an indication of a real change in the nature of Catholic development in England—a conclusion in which he was not mistaken. Between 1853 and 1862 there was a whole series of disputes between Wiseman and the bishops, each one, in reality, not about the apparent surface issues but concerned with resistance to the 'Roman' spirit inherent in Wiseman's conception of his office. Wiseman, in effect, at last introduced England to Tridentine Catholicism. To the exultant converts, anxious to luxuriate in everything which differentiated themselves from the English religion they had abandoned, this was splendid; to the Old Catholics, however, it was a lamentable and insensitive renunciation of a religious tone which echoed centuries of sacrifice and common-sense adjustment to Protestant sensibilities. The most notorious and divisive of Wiseman's disputes with the bishops began in 1858, and concerned the status of St Edmund's College, Ware: his appointment as Vice-President of Herbert Vaughan, who became one of the Oblates of St Charles founded by Manning the preceding year, was regarded as an attempt to hand the college over to ultramontane influences. The result was a protracted conflict with the Westminster Chapter. Errington took up the case for the traditional independence of the English colleges, and

Wiseman defended his attempts to introduce Roman discipline into the training of the priesthood. Both sides appealed to Rome, but it was not until 1863 that Propaganda eventually handed down a balanced judgement in which Wiseman's central contention was actually denied. The whole issue had meanwhile engendered an atmosphere of great tension within the leadership of the Church. (By 1862 this had become so noticeable that most of the bishops excused themselves from attendance at the annual Low Week meeting.) Wiseman had been determined to dispose of Errington. Errington had refused to go. Further appeals to Rome had proceeded, and in 1860 Errington had even defied a request made personally by Pius IX for him to accept the Archbishopric of Trinidad *in lieu* of the coadjutorship at Westminster. He was then dismissed by the Holy Father and retired to Prior Park, where he taught theology until his death in 1886.

In judging Wiseman's record of conflict in his Westminster years it is as well to remember the difficulties in which he was placed. The bishops had an established pattern of independent action, yet the Vatican was urging Wiseman to unify and centralize the Church. In Rome, before his English career began, Wiseman had a deserved reputation for diplomatic conduct, for excellence as a host, and for a sensible and courteous attitude to Protestants. In England, however, he was always in a small minority: his revolution in the Church—the decisive imprint of ultramontanism—was achieved with very few followers within the leadership. He was, additionally, increasingly given to debilitating illnesses, and this led to a dependence on Manning which was resented both because Manning was a junior convert and because he was an ultramontane zealot. Reliance on the Italian religious orders and the introduction of the new devotional practices were further occasions of local conflict between the leadership and the Old Catholics. Wiseman himself wrote two books of popular devotions for the laity; their emphasis lay in the cultivation of a popular piety similar to that of south European folk religion. It was all profoundly un-English, and, to those who resisted them, the new devotions appeared simply superstitious. Wiseman also gloried in the ecclesiastical miracles of the Counter-Reformation Church and in the cults of St Philip Neri and St Charles Borromeo. He placed relics in the chapels at Ushaw and St Edmund's. The Old Catholics were very shocked. They sensed that his clericalism would exalt the priesthood and depress the laity to the point at which they would lose all influence. Wiseman, for his part, saw the universal authority of papal monarchy as an essential barrier against the indifferentism and infidelity of the age, and although he was open to modern scholarship, as he understood it, he saw English Protestantism all round him sinking into liberalism and ultimate scepticism. The fault, he believed, lay in the very nature of the Church of England, the supposed guardian of Christian truth. For it was not, in his contention, a 'branch' of Christendom at all, but a limb amputated at the Reformation and incapable of revitalizing itself in the poisoned atmosphere of nineteenth-century intellectual culture. The proof of this seemed to be the Oxford Movement: those Anglicans who fell upon dogmatic principles of religion had felt obliged to leave their Church for they recognized its inherent incompatibility, as a national and local institution, with universal truth and the means by which it is defined and protected.

Like some European ultramontanists, Wiseman's mind embraced a mixture of ecclesiastical authoritarianism and liberal culture. He was far from the 'medievalism' of some of the converts, despite his personal friendship with Pugin, and in his self-conscious identification with English values it was the liberal political tradition which most attracted his sympathy. He was at home with the 'Steam Age mentality', gloried in the inventiveness of the times, and sought to attach Christianity to the expansive and progressive qualities of the intelligentsia. In his writings and sermons there was frequent reference to the essential compatibility of science and revealed truth, of religion and modern society. But as the liberal Protestant theologians began to abandon dogmatic principles and to incorporate a historical relativism into their view of scriptural authenticity, Wiseman began to draw back—not from his basic position, but he became more insistent in emphasizing the need for modern knowledge to be interpreted by ecclesiastical authority. He supported biblical accounts of the Creation. In later years he sensed some future conflict of ideas, in which religious truth would have to contend for its survival against a secularized culture. Wiseman's earlier political liberalism was also modified as the years passed. As a beneficiary of the reform process—which was how he regarded Catholic Emancipation—he adhered quietly to liberal politics. In public he avoided party allegiance until the 1850s, when the association of the Whigs with the anti-Catholic uproar over the restored hierarchy impelled him into Toryism. The support of liberals for the Italian *Risorgimento* confirmed his shifted allegiance, and in the 1859 elections he intervened on the Tory side at the Irish polls. In 1864 he condemned the visit to England of Garibaldi, whose reception by public men seemed to be an abandonment of principles of order, a national endorsement of foreign revolutionism. Though an advocate of the values of political economy, as most enlightened men of his time were, Wiseman was touched by an older sense of traditional social responsibility in his attitude to the poor. In Westminster he regarded himself as having a special pastoral vocation to the 'huge and almost countless population' in the slums of the capital. When he visited the courts and alleys of the London working class, which he did often, the poor pressed close to touch his robes. What they perceived in Wiseman was some spiritual quality far deeper than the superficial display of ecclesiastical grandeur in which he also exulted; what they sensed, as by instinct, was a real love of the poor and a confidence in the ennobling of present circumstance by the riches of eternity.

It is possible that Wiseman's understanding of Catholicism derived from an ephemeral episode in papal development—from the Italian religiosity of the States of the Church as described in his *Recollections of the Last Four Popes and of Rome in their Times*, published in 1858. Some have supposed that his imposition of ultramontane attitudes and practices did considerable injury to the existing traditions of English Catholicism. What is astonishing was his success in the policy he set himself in view of the very narrow base of support he enjoyed among the English Catholics. His reputation was a European one; amongst his own co-religionists he had no party and elicited no great sympathy. Doubtless the great expansiveness of Victorian Catholicism was anyway set to occur, due to the Irish influx and to existing trends within the English Church. Wiseman's ultramontane vision reaped credit for a dynamism that was, perhaps, already in evidence. The Victorian boom in religion would have affected the Catholics whatever the direction insisted upon from the top. Yet to Wiseman must belong the establishment of a public Catholic presence, and the inspiration of confidence in many humble people who saw a prince of the Church become acceptable to the Protestant nation. From what seemed the disaster of the Flaminian Gate Pastoral, Wiseman lived to see Catholicism made more or less respectable with many sections of opinion. He died in 1865, worn out and ill, his last years, in Manning's words, 'like the hours of a still afternoon, when the work of the day begins to linger, and the silence of evening is near'.

As Wiseman's successor at Westminster, Manning continued the diffusion of the ultramontane spirit and, through sound administration and more judicious use of authority than his predecessor, he achieved a unity within English Catholicism quite unknown before. Yet his reputation has suffered badly, largely through some unfortunate passages in his official biography by E. S. Purcell, a Catholic journalist who was a friend of Manning's. The book appeared in 1895, and printed correspondence and notes by Manning which disclosed the material details of business. Frank assessments of the suitability of men for positions in the Church, a consciousness of his own capabilities as the bearer of authentic 'Roman' policies, and attempts to elicit favourable opinions from the Holy See in issues which divided the English Catholics: all were set down in Purcell's study, and to the unperceptive reader they made Manning appear unduly consumed by personal ambition. This was very far from reality.

After Newman, Manning was the most important of the Anglican converts. Henry Edward Manning was born in Hertfordshire in 1807 and educated at Harrow. In Oxford, after 1827, he began to show what became a lifelong characteristic—political liberalism. He met Gladstone, who was slightly his junior, and the two began a friendship which, interrupted first through religious difference and then through opposed views on the temporal sovereignty of the papacy, was to last throughout their lives. Originally intending a political or commercial career, Manning returned to Oxford in 1832 and prepared for Holy Orders in the Church of England. There then began a successful pastoral ministry in Sussex, and in 1833 he married. But the death of his wife in 1837 seems to have initiated an internal transformation—for long unperceived in its implications —that led eventually to his disillusionment with Anglicanism. In the desolation of his loneliness, he sought in the early Fathers and in the Caroline divines some surer basis for his faith than the conventional evangelicalism he had until then professed. His doctrine of the Church began to change, as he sensed something of the spiritual autonomy necessary for true religious authority. After two visits to Rome, and influenced by the new forces emanating from Oxford, his unsettlement was greatly enhanced by the Gorham Judgment of 1850, which he took to confirm very starkly what he had for so long supposed inwardly: that the Church of England lacked spiritual integrity through its union with the liberal modern State. In 1851 he joined the Catholic Church.

Manning was by then forty-one years old. His vocation continued to be to the priesthood and he was almost at once ordained by Wiseman, and sent off to study at the Accademia Ecclesiastica in Rome. In 1854 he returned to serve in London and in 1857 founded the Oblates of St Charles in Bayswater. In the same year he was appointed Provost of the Chapter of Westminster by Pius IX. It was an astonishing rise to immediate influence in the Church and caused some ill-feeling amongst those who had for long been labouring in the vineyard. In 1865 he became Archbishop, and in 1875 was made a Cardinal. Like Wiseman, who came to depend upon his administrative abilities, Manning was an isolated figure in the Church. He lacked natural connections with the Old Catholic families, and his developing social interests were not in general shared by his brother clerics. His ultramontanism was exact and many thought rigid. His intellectual interests were wide, however, and he wrote with a deceptive simplicity a number of short works which had great spiritual depth, especially *The Eternal Priesthood*, published in 1883. He was close to Vaughan, whom he first met as a student in Rome, and consulted Bishop Cornthwaite; yet his direction of affairs was inevitably single-handed. He undoubtedly sought to further his own cause as Wiseman's successor, but his motive here was essentially religious and not personal: he was intensely anxious that the leadership of the Church should not revert to the pre-ultramontane 'English' figures who were the obvious candidates—Clifford, Errington, or Grant. Hence the mediation of Mgr. George Talbot with the Roman authorities on his behalf. Talbot, another convert, appeared frequently at the Roman end of English Catholic affairs in the nineteenth century. He had become a papal chamberlain and was one of the most trusted advisers of Pius IX personally (his influence with Propaganda was very much less). He and Manning maintained a close connection until Talbot's illness in 1869 led to his permanent retirement from Rome.

The ultramontane centre of Manning's Catholicism was first seen publicly in 1860 when he gave a series of sermons on the temporal power of the papacy. This defence—against the advancing forces of the Garibaldians in Italy—was subsequently published, together with some other lectures on the subject, in a book. Manning defended the temporal sovereignty as essential to the spiritual independence of the universal Church; he regarded the States of the Church as a direct trust from God himself. It was a view which, though conventional enough in papal and some European circles, was not initially popular with the Old Catholics, with all their traditional reservations about papal monarchy. In later life Manning came to recognize the reality of change in Italy, and made himself for a time distasteful to the Court of Leo XIII by urging an accommodation with the kingdom of Italy. As a champion of papal views of Catholicism, he was at his most influential at the Vatican Council, and took a considerable part in arranging the events which led to the definition of infallibility in 1870. This, too, distanced him from the 'Inopportunist' English Catholics, and especially from Clifford and Errington. He had an almost apocalyptic sense that the civilized world, for so long sustained by Christianity, was sliding into chaos; a sense that some great catastrophe for humanity was impending. Catholic unity, centralized in the papacy, was the only means, he believed, for Christendom to survive: the battle was against the relativizing intellectual forces of the age, with their tendency to exalt individualism and indifferentism. His support for the *Syllabus of Errors* in 1864 was precisely because it met the evils of the day head-on. The Church, to be the centre of unity and the guardian of human freedom, must be independent of the civil powers. It alone, and not secular ethicism, could determine what was true in moral order, in the nature of man and his purpose in the world. Difficulties between himself and Newman, which were evident to both men throughout their lives, derived in some measure from their different attitudes to the intellectual culture of their times. Newman, too, feared the effects for religion of the secularizing assault upon dogma, but unlike Manning, who sought to hold things down through ecclesiastical authority, Newman probed the processes of historical change and sought some prophetic insight into the means by which the religious truth it conveyed could be identified and activated. Newman, that is to say, ultimately regarded the development of culture as progressive; Manning saw the modern world as the departure from a permanent standard of truth.

Manning's ultramontane scepticism about the modern State was in curious contrast to his actual attitude to evolving liberal government in England. For Manning was not only a self-conscious liberal in politics, he also came to espouse a vision of social reform which required State activity. Like many of the leading churchmen of the Anglican Establishment, he came to espouse a critique of classical political economy and a belief in the propriety of limited government enterprise in the alleviation of social evils. In 1889 he declared: 'My watchword is, For God and the People.' He was, in fact, more radical than Gladstone, and more prepared for social reform, but it was to be change within the social system. Manning's liberalism did not envisage basic social class transformations. From 1867 he supported the United Kingdom Alliance, the great temperance movement of the Dissenters whose radical political purposes were not disguised. He also endorsed trade-unionism, and especially the union movement of the agricultural labourers. He mediated in the dock strike of 1889, plainly on the side of labour. This, also, was at variance with 'Gladstonian' free-contract ideas. Manning believed that the Catholic Church should support the people; the Anglicans had made the mistake of allowing their Church to become a class institution. In 1890 he wrote: 'The rich can take care of themselves, and their underlings can help them', and 'My politics are social politics.' It was not at all what the surviving Old Catholic families were accustomed to hearing from their bishop. Manning was not, however, a socialist. He retained an enormous suspicion of European socialism, so strongly condemned in the *Syllabus* of 1864, and regarded it as a harbinger of total government. He also disapproved of party political allegiance both for himself and for the clergy. An exception came in 1884 when he advised the Catholic voters to support the party of denominational education (the Conservatives), but he regarded this as an expedient directed to religious, not political, purposes. His most important social state-ment, *The Dignity and Rights of Labour*, a lecture delivered to the Leeds Mechanics' Institute in 1874, was innocent of party politics. It was a close criticism of *laissez-faire* practices. 'I claim for labour the rights of property', he said. He defended the right of working people to organize for better wages and conditions. It was not an inventive or even unusual position; but it was rare to hear it publicly expressed, in mid-Victorian England, by a Roman Catholic Archbishop. Some writers have attributed Leo XIII's social encyclical letters and especially *Rerum Novarum* (1891) to Manning's influence, but this is not likely; Manning's reputation at Rome was not, by then, very considerable—rather the reverse, owing to his attitude on Italian politics—and Rome had, anyway, a European body of ideas to hand as its major source.

Not all of Manning's social interests were merely declaratory. He was an activist not only in the temperance movement but in a number of Mansion House committees for social and charitable enterprises, and in 1884 he was appointed to serve on the Royal Commission of inquiry into the condition of working-class housing. Between 1887 and 1888 he was a member of the Committee on Distress in London. He also worked for antivivisectionist groups and in support of systematic emigration as a form of social relief for the poor. Like all Catholic bishops, he was concerned with popular education. His first three Pastoral Letters as Archbishop were devoted to the need for more Catholic schools, and he laid aside plans to construct a London cathedral in order to promote the financing of schools. In 1866 he set up the Westminster Diocesan Education Fund to manage the campaign he was initiating. His feelings for the poor were reciprocated, and when he died, in 1892, there were quite extraordinary scenes of popular mourning. Thousands of ordinary people, many of them Protestants, paid a last tribute at Archbishop's House, their sense of Manning's spiritual care somehow penetrating the traditional religious barriers of centuries. Trade unionists carried banners in the funeral procession. 'A great light of the Church has gone out,' Pope Leo XIII said on hearing of Manning's death; ' I feel that my own hour is at hand.' To have joined Catholicism to public life in the way Manning had done was a very remarkable achievement: the most ultramontane of prelates had been acclaimed by the most Protestant of peoples.

Though lighter in weight than Wiseman and Manning, at least in learning and influence upon the public consciousness, Herbert Vaughan was more than their equal in one important contribution to Catholic expansion: he was a skilled and even inspired administrator, whose stamp upon the English Catholic Church could be discerned for more than half a century. Though the son of an Old Catholic family, his ultramontanism was as decided as Manning's. He was a grand-nephew of Cardinal Weld, and was born of Herefordshire landowning stock in 1832. Destined by his father for a military career, Vaughan fell under the evidently more forceful direction of his mother and entered the priesthood. All five of the daughters of the family became nuns, and six of the eight sons became priests. In 1841 Vaughan was sent to Stonyhurst, and in 1851, after brief periods at Downside and at the Jesuit school at Brugelette in Belgium, he left for Rome to commence study for the priesthood. He was ordained in 1854 and was then, at the age of only twenty-three, given the Vice-Presidency of St Edmund's College by Wiseman. Recognized by the other staff of the college as the precursor of an ultramontane assault, his appointment precipitated the row which became the central upheaval of Wiseman's reign at Westminster. It was during this period of unsettlement that Vaughan conceived the idea of founding a missionary society, with the vision of matching the great English Protestant missions overseas, a feature of the century, with an English Catholic counterpart. After a fund-raising expedition to North and South America in 1863, the enterprise was begun. The St Joseph's Missionary Society, with its college at Mill Hill, established in 1866, was Vaughan's first essay in administrative work, and it was an enormous success. The first missionaries left in 1871 for work among the black populations of North American cities. In 1879 a parallel society for women was set up. The missionaries Vaughan trained were filled with the 'Roman' spirit. His other early contribution to the supremacy of ultramontanism in the Church was in Catholic journalism. In 1868 he purchased the *Tablet* and used it to promote the ideals of loyalty to Rome and ecclesiastical authority. In 1878 he bought the *Dublin Review* as well. From its pages, also, non-Roman sentiments were rigorously excluded.

Vaughan was not a scholar and his grasp of intellectual categories was not great. He was a little humourless but much dedicated. The gentler side of his nature was hidden from the world—but disclosed to Lady Herbert of Lea, the widow of the War Minister in Lord Aberdeen's government, whom he first met in 1866 and with whom he enjoyed a close and moving confidence until the end of his life. She assisted his work with financial contributions and sound advice. But his clergy found him cold and distant. A large part of his time, in fact, was given to the work—to him 'hateful'—of raising money for his various enterprises: for his missions, for education, for 'rescue' work among the poor. He was not as inflexible as his austere public image suggested. He believed in vernacular services, and in the adaptation of the Church to national life. There was, in this second conviction, no hint of 'Gallicanism': the Church was to see itself as having a mission to the whole nation and not merely to Catholics. The great symbol of this was his building of Westminster Cathedral, begun soon after his arrival in London as Manning's successor. It was a monument to ultramontanism, to the triumphalist note as addressed to the English people, constructed in the manner of a Roman basilica, in the Byzantine style. Vaughan's adherence to the strictest notions of the 'Roman spirit' was also evident in his complete lack of sympathy for the ideas of reunion (canvassed from 1894) between the Anglican and the Catholic Churches. These were the work of the Abbé Fernand Portal and Lord Halifax. Though they represented only a very small body of opinion in either Church, Leo XIII was persuaded that the Anglicans were on the point of submission to the Holy See, and it took all of Vaughan's skill, assisted by Gasquet and Merry del Val, to persuade him otherwise. In 1895 he set up a committee of Catholic theologians to examine the case for reunion, and in the following year the Vatican appointed an international commission for the same purpose. The validity of Anglican orders was by then perceived to be the central issue. Vaughan used all his influence against recognition, and was upheld in the bull of 1896, *Apostolicae Curae*. His view of the Church, and the work of his two great predecessors at Westminster, was preserved.

Part of Vaughan's separation from the clergy resulted from his more or less permanent poor health, which meant that such time as he had for work was allocated to his administrative duties. He was also unable to surmount the social manners and outlook of his landed background, and found visiting the poor in their homes —which he did with dedication—an enormous personal strain. He was a conservative in politics, one of the few things in which he differed from his great friend and patron, Manning. The work of the Church, he believed, conventionally enough, should be free of party politics and should be essentially pastoral and charitable rather than related to, or supportive of, general humanitarianism within public life. There was here, also, a shade of difference from Manning. Yet it was Vaughan who founded the Social Union clubs in London's East End. They were for youth recreation among the working classes, and by 1894 there were five of them, already beginning to show the same enthusiasm for social reformism that the Anglican 'settlements' in the slums had done. Unlike Manning, Vaughan had no interest in Irish political issues, and this, too, cut him off from a sympathetic contact with large sections of the Irish Catholics of the parishes.

When the diocese of Salford fell vacant in 1872, the choice of Vaughan as successor to Bishop Turner was controversial. He owed it to Manning's influence, for he was relatively unknown in the powerful Catholic Church of the north, most of whose leaders came from Ushaw. But the work there was exactly suited to Vaughan's administrative capabilities, and he built upon his predecessor's educational foundations to inaugurate a period of rapid expansion. A pastoral seminary for the training of priests in urban work was opened in 1874; diocesan synods became annual and were converted into bodies for the co-ordination of fund-raising for church building and 'rescue' work: forty new parishes were created in his time as bishop. He released some of the secondary education from the control of the religious orders; this involved the conflict with the Jesuits which led to *Romanos Pontifices* in 1881. But it was the 'rescue' work which took up more and more of the centre of his episcopate. On arrival in Salford Vaughan had been impressed by the huge numbers, so it seemed, who 'leaked' from the faith, through clerical negligence, through bad social conditions, and through lack of Catholic education. What was required, first, was some sort of statistical evidence as to the dimensions of the problem: in 1884 he got his Chapter to set up a board of inquiry for this purpose, and a census of the diocese, on a parish basis, took place. Quite apart from the immediate value of the returns, the whole undertaking gave the clergy first-hand information about the social conditions of their people. On the basis of the findings, in 1886 Vaughan founded the Catholic Protection and Rescue Society, to save the faith of Catholic children by providing alternative social relief from that given by the workhouses and the Protestant philanthropic bodies. The laity were mobilized in the work, and this was one of Vaughan's most important achievements. By the time he left Salford some two thousand Catholic laymen were involved in social work. He carried the work to London, too, and in 1894 a census was carried out there. In 1899 the 'Crusade of Rescue' was set up on a national basis.

The move to Westminster as Manning's successor came in 1892, when Vaughan was sixty. This time his appointment was not controversial; he was the obvious person to lead the Church. In 1893 he was made a cardinal. As well as the 'rescue' work, he was particularly active in educational questions while in London. Manning's policy of excluding Catholics from the ancient universities was abandoned; the Hammersmith seminary he had set up was transferred to Oscott. Vaughan also presented the Catholic case over denominational schools to the Government and to the public. His success, in this last area, came with the Education Act of 1902, in which Catholics achieved parity with the Protestant schools in maintenance grants. Vaughan said that 'his last work was done'. It had been extraordinarily impressive work, not only in educational questions but in the general supervision of the Catholic Church, which ended the nineteenth century, as a consequence of his labours, with an efficient and expansive machinery. Despite the wooden formality which those who met Vaughan sensed, his life was marked by interior suffering as well as by actual bodily ill-health. This did not abate, even at the end. He died in 1903, meeting eventual serenity, but only after fearful anguish and a supervening consciousness of his own spiritual frailty.

As well as this line of great ecclesiastical leaders, the English Catholic Church of the nineteenth century also had some distinguished scholars and thinkers. Indeed, in Cardinal Newman it had the most celebrated English Catholic of modern times. Yet Newman was not in any institutional sense a Catholic leader—his Catholic life was spent entirely in the Birmingham Oratory which he founded. Apart from the visits to Dublin in the 1850s to conduct the affairs of the Catholic University of which he was Rector, he remained an isolated figure, away from the mainstream of ecclesiastical business, holding no office, and as much distrusted by many of his new Catholic superiors as he had been by his Anglican ones. But men were never unaware of his existence. Newman's opinions were sought on crucial issues of Christian polity, and his indirect influence on the climate of opinion in the Church of his day was very considerable.

It was Newman's conversion in 1845 that contemporaries regarded as a decisive marker in Catholic resurgence. His life, however, had about it a measure of consistency which that apparently enormous change obscured. It was a long life. John Henry Newman was born in London, the son of a banker, in 1801, and he died in 1890. He was educated at a school in Ealing, and then, after 1817, at Trinity College, Oxford. In 1822 he became a fellow of Oriel College and sought holy orders. As Vicar of St Mary's after 1828, he preached the sermons which the most recent academic authority on his life, Professor Owen Chadwick, has described as his 'chief work'. The first of the six published volumes appeared in 1834. He was greatly influenced by his study of the early Fathers, deriving from them a subtle spirituality and also a sense of religious authority which was centred in dogma, properly understood, and universal consensus. His contributions to the *Tracts for the Times*—he wrote twenty-four in the series—reflected his desire to see the Church of England revitalized according to these Catholic principles. Most of the Anglican bishops were unimpressed and in their own charges denounced the *Tracts*. This placed Newman in a dilemma: his central appeal was to the authority of the Church, yet the authorities of his own Church were patently hostile to the conception of the Church he espoused. In the midst of his unsettlement he retired to Littlemore in 1842, and a quasi-monastic life developed among the few friends who joined him there. In September 1843 he resigned from St Mary's, and in 1845 was received into the Catholic Church.

Newman had very little notion of the actual Catholic Church in England to which he adhered. His conversion was not a discontinuity of ideas, but of circumstance and allegiances. His view of the Church remained the same, his conversion indicating that he regarded the Church of the Fathers as being embodied in Catholicism and not in the Church of England. Anglicanism, in fact, he had come to recognize as a modern counterpart to the early heresies he had studied—a conviction which had begun to grow from around 1832, when he published his *Arians of the Fourth Century*. The whole idea of a 'national' Church, and especially one subject to Erastian control in an apostatizing State, was contrary to the universal authority of antiquity. Newman therefore developed an ideal of the Church in isolation from any particular school of thought, and it was this that led him to Catholicism. He owed very few intellectual debts, and remained intellectually isolated all his life.

Hence the extent of his religious genius. There were, of course, early contributors to his thinking. At Oriel, Edward Hawkins had taught him that the Scriptures needed to be interpreted within ecclesiastical tradition, an ideal greatly at variance with the received evangelicalism to which Newman had before looked. From Richard Whately he acquired a distrust of Erastianism. From Richard Hurrell Froude he gained an insight into Catholic devotional sensitivity, even though Froude, too, was an Anglican. Wiseman supplied the last crucial ingredient. In 1839 Newman read his article on the Donatist heresy in the *Dublin Review* and was stunned by the implications of St Augustine's words *securus judicat orbis terrarum*. The Church of England seemed almost hopelessly outside the universal circle of faith: it lacked apostolical authenticity. He had seen, as he later recorded, 'the shadow of a hand upon the wall'. As a Catholic after 1845 his view of the Church did not change.

The independence and isolation of Newman's mind did not mean that others avoided seeking to claim his authority for their own party positions. Within the Catholic Church most of the opponents of ultramontanism, whether Old Catholic or liberal, sought to identify him as a supporter. But as an Anglican he had tried to keep clear of parties and as a Catholic he certainly did so. Nor was he concerned with politics. There was always in him a sort of Tory paternalism, and, as became painfully apparent in the Dublin Catholic University, he had a set of prejudices about the styles of gentlemanly life which Catholicism did nothing to modify. Yet he regarded politics as a very secondary affair, unsatisfactory because it substituted impersonal categories for the real personal relationships in which human experience was encountered and dignified. He regarded the spiritual state of men in his day as in much more urgent need of attention than their material condition. Despite his association with the *Rambler*—the liberal journal of the converts, which he edited in 1859 and consistently defended against ultramontane attacks —Newman was not in any ordinary sense a 'liberal Catholic' either. He had a basic belief in the moral limitations of men, and did not regard the social order as potentially or actually progressive. He was very far removed from the contentions of those, like Acton, who supposed that the establishment of an enlightened political order would further the ends of Christianity. In his opposition to the temporal power of the papacy, and in his 'minimalistic' interpretation of papal infallibility, he was certainly close to positions also occupied by the liberal Catholics, but his reasons for arriving at these attitudes were far from theirs. It was crucial to Newman's general outlook that Christianity and knowledge were compatible: that a proper understanding of the relationship between the faith and evolving cultural forms was the beginning of an insight into religious truth. The liberal Catholics and the later 'modernists', however, sought to reconcile Catholicism and contemporary knowledge: there was an important difference here, for they accepted the integrity of modern knowledge, and the secular value–structure which sustained it, without recognizing the disguised values which it also incorporated. They were critical of the past, that is to say, and not of the present. Newman saw all things committed to change, and was moved by a real sense of the importance of dogma as providing criteria with which to evaluate the transformations in both religious and secular perceptions of the world. In Rome to receive the cardinal's hat in 1879, Newman summarized his lifelong resistance to liberalism: 'the doctrine that there is no positive truth in religion, but that one creed is as good as another'.

Yet with the liberal Catholicism of the second half of the century, Newman had much more in common than might at first appear. His view of the relationship between ecclesiastical authority and intellectual enquiry was more subtle than that of the leading liberals. He believed in authority; they did not. He saw it abused by the ultramontanes, in their process of clericalizing the Church. In a famous article on the role of the laity in the definition of Christian truth, in the *Rambler* of July 1859, he envisaged a widely diffused basis to ecclesiastical authority: in the Arian controversy of the fourth century the bishops had erred while the laity remained orthodox. This was not the sort of evidence that was most agreeable to the ultramontanes, and it helped to keep Newman out of favour with Rome. Ideas, he believed, had to be tested within the whole community of the faithful. He was sceptical of 'intellectualism', of elevating theoretical concepts above revelation, for the truths of revelation were available to all who sought them. Guided by the consensus of those who have gone before—by 'tradition' and ecclesiastical 'authority'—authentic belief could be established. In 1870 he said, 'The Church moves as a whole; it is not a mere philosophy, it is a communion.' The most important statement of

Newman's view of the relationship between ideas, historical sequences, and the formulation of religious doctrine came while he was still an Anglican, and was published just after his conversion. The *Essay on the Development of Christian Doctrine* projected a subtle sense of human discernment: religious development is according to the same sort of historical and material influences as produce all change. Revealed truth is transmitted through human agency and is therefore subjected to circumstance. The Christian life involves seeking the means of recognizing the components in the mixture for what they are and in defining the areas of their authority. The book illustrated and advanced Newman's essential conviction that all life is change, and that men cannot become external to their own involvement with the stuff of reality. Development, however, can show continuities, and Catholic teachings not found in antiquity —Marian devotions or papal monarchy, for example—can be seen as fruits of the process. Newman was not a dialectician, and stood in the English tradition of empirical thinking: the idea of development valued tradition yet placed it upon a shifting basis; it recognized the relativity of human investments in what were incorrectly regarded as immutable expressions of truth while it saw an essential deposit of revealed knowledge at the centre; it appreciated the corruption of institutions while it found permanency in a universal perception of authentic apostolic doctrine. The book was denounced in Rome by Perrone, the most celebrated theologian in the city, and was not popular with the English Catholic leaders. It was probably more appreciated by Protestants. Newman's old teacher, Whately, acutely remarked that it was more likely to turn men into sceptics than Romanists.

Rome persisted in regarding Newman with considerable reserve for many years. Manning and the ultramontane party were doubtful if he was a real Catholic at all, and were additionally suspicious of the affinity with his position claimed by the Old Catholic remnant. The publication of the *Apologia* in 1864, in which Newman movingly and honestly retraced the steps of his conversion to the Catholic Church, was not liked by the ultramontanes, who felt it treated Anglicanism as if it was capable of authentic spirituality. But the book rehabilitated him with large areas of Protestant opinion, impressed by its fairness and sensitivity. Rome, too, began to reconsider. In 1869 Newman was invited to attend the Vatican Council as an advisory theologian by several bishops. He declined, because of age, and because he was working on his *Grammar of Assent* at the time. In 1879 he was made a cardinal by Leo XIII. 'The cloud is lifted from me for ever', he said. As Newman was not the product of a single school of thought so he did not found one either, though his ideas have had an enormous number of interpreters since his death. The impression of his religious thinking presented here does adequate justice neither to the breadth of his writings nor to their fine analytical distinctions. Newman was also a man of personal sanctity and hidden depths of spiritual discernment; he offered up the solitary desolations of his life and received, in return, extraordinary treasures of religious enlightenment.

The other great intellectual contribution made by the Oxford Movement to the Catholic Church was William George Ward. In 1845 the convocation of Oxford University condemned his book, *The Ideal of a Christian Church*, for Romish tendencies and Ward, who did not really deny them, crossed over the line so emphatically placed before him. He became a rich man and, on giving up his Anglican orders on conversion, he entered into the life of an independent lay scholar. With the learning of Winchester, Christ Church and Balliol behind him, he brought into his new Church a formidable intellect and a trained mind. From 1851 to 1858 he was Professor of Dogmatic Theology at St Edmund's College, and throughout the 1860s he edited the *Dublin Review*. He adhered to an extreme ultramontanism, and employed the journal to provide an inflexible justification for strict papalist attitudes, especially over the question of infallibility. He denied liberal Catholic positions with authority and style: Ward was a polemical writer of distinction and he enjoyed public controversy. In 1869 he became a respected member of the Metaphysical Society, and until John Stuart Mill's death in 1873 he maintained a correspondence given over exclusively to intellectual exchange.

As an exponent of ecclesiastical authority, centralized and defined, Ward was clearly considerably removed from Newman's position. Whereas Newman valued authority where it was truly the authority of religious truth expressed through the general assent of believers, Ward saw authority as the directive machinery of holiness, as the formal structure to which assent was made by those removed from its inner mysteries. From de Maistre Ward derived the notion that truth could only be preserved if the papacy itself laid down the intellectual basis upon which it could be established. The culture of the age, in his vision, tended to rationalism and secularism, and he regarded a permanent warfare between the Church and modern learning as an essential sign that religious authority was aware of the dangers. Yet there were no real political consequences of this scheme of things: Ward was not a political traditionalist, out to preserve the old world for fear of change. He disliked liberalism, for in Italy its agents were assailing the States of the Church, and in England the Gladstonians were applauding them. He distrusted the Tories with that high-minded detachment which most Victorian intellectuals had for what some characterized as 'the stupid party'. His chief weapons were directed against the Catholic liberals. He regarded the *Syllabus of Errors* as an infallible statement, and carried his understanding of infallibility so far, indeed, that in his *Authority of Doctrinal Decisions*, published in 1866, he enlarged its range to encompass all religious guidance given by the Pope, whether publicly or in private correspondence. This interpretation was confirmed in *De Infallibilitatis Extensione* of 1869, a work which showed Ward's affinity to Louis Veuillot. Newman opposed the book, as did Ullathorne (for the older English Catholic tradition). The Vatican Council itself, in its 1870 Decree on Infallibility, was much more circumspect. Ward himself, from around that time, was increasingly unwell, and in 1871 he retired to the Isle of Wight. More preoccupied now with philosophical than with theological speculation, he came to concede that some of his earlier opinions had been too extreme; he had pressed too far, as he put it, in 'the heat of polemics'. He must nevertheless be judged to have been a major influence in nineteenth-century English Catholic thinking, producing a systematic expression of the dominant ideals of the ultramontane leaders. He died in 1882.

Lord Acton, by contrast, was a thorn in the side of the bishops, and his influence within his own Church was slight. He was, nevertheless, one of the most important Catholic intellectual figures of the century, whose name has endured and whose contribution to modern historical scholarship is still apparently valued by many. Acton's influence in his lifetime was mostly with Protestant scholars and savants. His frequent and sharp rejections of ecclesiastical authority placed him far beyond the circles of the ultramontane leadership, and rather beyond what most ordinary Catholics, had they been aware of them, would have considered loyal or proper. Action revelled in it. He told the electors at the Bridgnorth election of 1865 that he belonged 'rather to the soul than the body of the Catholic Church', and it was not an inaccurate observation. His writings were irradiated with denunciations of former popes as 'murderers', and he enjoyed pointing to discreditable scandals in the Curia; he threw up what he supposed were historical evidences to show the inconsistencies of ecclesiastical authority. His family was an old Shropshire one, which had been converted to Catholicism in the preceding century, but Acton was born in Naples, where his father was on a diplomatic posting, in 1834. He succeeded to the baronetcy in 1837. His education was unorthodox: first in Paris, then Oscott, then in Edinburgh, and finally a six-year period of study in Munich under Döllinger. It was this last stretch which converted him to the supposition, which he retained all his life, that historical study provided the explanation of all knowledge.

There was a Whiggish reverence for the British Constitution in Acton's politics, and he actually sat in Parliament, as a Liberal, for ten years after 1859. In 1869 Gladstone rewarded him with a peerage. He believed that Christianity must be committed to the politics of liberty, and therefore deplored the ultramontanism of his day as an expression of ecclesiastical absolutism. He saw the Church, properly directed, as the great force able to counter the despotism of the State. The Munich Congress of 1863, and Montalembert's enunciation of the principles of religious and civil liberty, he regarded as 'the dawn of a new era'. Though originally a defender of papal temporal sovereignty, he came to attack it because of the illiberal political institutions of the papal states. The *Syllabus* he thought a straight denial of the progressive ideals which were making for a better world. He used his influence behind the scenes at the Vatican Council, which he witnessed by residing in Rome during some of its sessions, to try to persuade the powers to intervene and break it up—so avoiding the definition of infallibility. In that, he persuaded at least Gladstone. Yet Acton had no affinity with Newman: perhaps further indication, if any is needed, of how far Newman really was from the liberal Catholic position. In 1880 Acton called him an 'evil' man, and in 1896, returning to the theme, he dismissed his religious opinions as 'a school of Infidelity'. He had correctly discerned Newman's essential maintenance of dogmatic principles. 'Newman professed liberalism', he said, 'when in fact he was in favour of the Inquisition.' By then Acton was given over to an academic career, appointed, through Lord Rosebery's influence, to the Regius Chair of Modern History at Cambridge. There he set himself to the editing of the *Cambridge Modern History* and to the planning of a vast and definitive History of Liberty, no part of which ever appeared. He died in 1902. However greatly he was at variance with the Catholicism of his day, Acton's importance for the Catholics lay in the sheer example of his public life. To have provided a regius professor within the same century as Catholic Emancipation was no small thing for the Church.

The ecclesiastical authorities and the intellectuals had disagreed before. A series of controversies over the *Rambler* brought matters to a head in the mid-century. This journal was started by John Moore Capes, a convert Anglican clergyman, in 1848, and in 1857 Acton became part-proprietor and Richard Simpson, another Anglican convert, became editor. The *Rambler* was noted for free intellectual enquiry, and as the vehicle of liberal opinion. It was also closely associated with the converts, and its occasionally dismissive references to the educational levels of most traditional English Catholics caused a great deal of offence. The *Rambler* was therefore disliked because of its intellectual tone by the Old Catholics and by the ultramontane leadership because of its disregard of ecclesiastical authority. Newman's brief editorship, in 1859, was at the initiative of Wiseman, Ullathorne, and Grant, who hoped that he would be a moderating influence. In the event his own essay 'On Consulting the Faithful in matters of Doctrine' merely added fuel to the fire. Sensing that ecclesiastical censure was at hand—for the bishops were frequently complaining to Propaganda about its articles—the journal changed its name to the *Home and Foreign Review* in 1862. Its general style, however, was unaltered, and the authorities were unsatisfied. In 1864 it ceased publication voluntarily, rather than face formal ecclesiastical censure.

For some English Catholics, as for some elsewhere in the world, it was the Vatican Council which also raised fears for intellectual freedom. The doctrine of papal infallibility, which rapidly emerged as the major theme shortly after the commencement of the sessions in 1869, had been implied in Catholic thinking for centuries, but the circumstances of the definition, in the wash of ultramontane triumphalism, appeared to many liberal Catholics to indicate wider threats to the maintenance of their attitudes. Ward's exaggerations of infallibility also did nothing to lessen their fears. Of the English bishops, Errington and Clifford tended to complete theological objection to the doctrine but never formally declared against it, while a central group, through not actually 'inopportunists', had substantial doubts about the advisability of a definition. Ullathorne, Grant, and Cornthwaite supported Manning's influential endorsement of infallibility. Liberal opinion in England, among both Catholics and Protestants, was made even more uneasy by the hostile and inaccurate reporting of events in Rome by the *Times* correspondent, Thomas Mozley, an Anglican clergyman who was Newman's brother-in-law. Gladstone's pamphlet assault upon the Vatican Decrees, in 1874, led to a lively public controversy, and to replies by (among others) Manning and Newman. Gladstone's contention was that the Council's work amounted to an attack upon modern ideas and government. 'No one can now become her convert', he wrote of the Catholic Church, 'without renouncing his moral and mental freedom.' Newman's reply became a characteristically sober and sensitive defence of conscience.

The last important issue between the authorities and some sections of Catholic intellectual opinion came with the modernists at the end of the century. The 'crisis' associated with their claims to freedom of religious thought really belongs to the first part of the twentieth century, but the battle-lines were drawn up by Leo XIII's encyclical of 1893, *Providentissimus Deus*, which indicated the need for theological scholarship to be subject to the *magisterium* of the Church. Acton was a modernist, in the sense that he claimed certain areas as the preserve of intellectual enquiry set upon terms of reference provided by the world of learning itself and not by religious authority. But it was Baron Friedrich von Hügel whose challenges to the bishops were more immediately threatening, or so they supposed, to authority. He was the son of an Austrian diplomat, and never lost a Germanic moral seriousness. From the Abbé Henri Huvelin he derived the lifelong insistence that conscience was more important than orthodoxy. He was not opposed to the spiritual authority of the papacy, but to the representation of nineteenth-century ultramontanism as a final and stable expression of it. He sought, in fact, a pre-Tridentine form of Catholicism, a return to collegiality in the Church. His critical writings, which began in the 1890s, emphasized the mystical rather than the institutional basis of Christian belief. His friend George Tyrrell was more extreme. He was a converted Irish Protestant, who in 1880 became a Jesuit. By the later 1890s, however, his writings indicated a marked departure from orthodoxy, and a searing rejection of ecclesiastical authority. In 1907 he was deprived of the sacraments. St George Jackson Mivart was another convert who quarrelled with the leadership. He was a lawyer and scientist whose biological research was wholly acceptable to the Church—Pius IX awarded him a doctorate in 1876—but whose identification of the soul with human rationality, and whose pursuit of complete freedom of the conscience and the intellect from ecclesiastical control, drew him into conflict with the bishops. Some of his works, published in 1892–3, were condemned by the Holy Office. Mivart himself lapsed into a version of theism. Victorian Catholicism certainly did not lack intellectual vitality. Controversy within the contemporaneous Protestant churches was largely about scriptural authority: they lacked the effective ecclesiastical machinery which made Catholic disputes unavoidably institutional in nature. At the end of the century, however, Catholicism in England was disclosing numerous signs of healthy growth, of which these disputes within Catholic intellectual circles were perhaps a minor by-product.

6 Twentieth-century developments

The centralized, clericalized, disciplined Church fashioned under ultramontane influence in the nineteenth century lasted until well into the middle of the succeeding one. As the English bishops left for the Second Vatican Council, in the autumn of 1962, most were aware of new attitudes in relations with the non-Catholic churches, and of progressively more open dispositions towards Catholicism within general society, but none of them was conscious that the whole pattern of authority within the Church itself was about to be altered. Cardinal Heenan, recalling his own unpreparedness for the change —which he came to welcome—declared that as Bishop of Leeds, from 1951, 'I was to do my duty by giving orders and the priests theirs by carrying them out.' The same economy of consultation was evident in the localities. In his study of a Liverpool working-class parish in 1957 (*Priests and People: A study in the sociology of religion*), Dr C. K. Ward noticed how the unquestioned authority of the priest fostered a hierocratic spirit and a church which was more evident in its structure than in its sense of community. 'The loyalty which existed appeared to be directed upwards, so to speak, towards the institution itself rather than in a horizontal direction towards the individuals of whom the parish was composed', he wrote. 'There was little evidence of any general consciousness of obligations of solidarity towards other parishioners.' The leadership at the centre in these years was characterized by administrative skill and the encouragement of devotional practice rather than by the sort of scholarly enterprise to which many of the nineteenth-century bishops had been given. Cardinal Bourne, who succeeded Vaughan in 1903 at Westminster, wrote just one book, a short treatise on ecclesiastical training, and his successor in 1935, Cardinal Hinsley, did not write a book at all. After the traumas associated with the condemnation of the ideas of the modernists, at the very start of the new century, Catholic learning in England had anyway passed into something of a quiescent phase. After the Council there was to be a considerable change in intellectual styles, as well as in ecclesiastical administration. So it may properly be said that English Catholic history divided off into a new segment somewhere in the 1960s. It would be unwise, even so, to exaggerate the impact of the division upon Catholic life in general, however. An opinion poll survey of 1978 revealed that 46 per cent of English Catholics had never heard of the Second Vatican Council.

In institutional terms, the ecclesiastical autonomy of the English Church was completed early in the twentieth century. Under the Apostolic Constitution *Sapienti Consilio*, of 1908, England and Wales ceased to be missionary districts subject to the jurisdiction of Propaganda; and with the publication of the code of Canon Law in 1918 existing 'missions' became regularly constituted parishes. These changes actually assisted that shift of emphasis, from the parishes to the dioceses, which became a marked feature of the Church during the first half of the century. Such residual local control as existed as a legacy from the 'gentry' past now disappeared altogether. The structure of centralization was itself revised. The bull *Si Qua Est*, in 1911, created two new provinces, under the Archbishops of Liverpool and Birmingham, alongside the province of Westminster. In 1916 Wales was constituted as a province under an Archbishop, with the diocese of Menevia as a suffragan see. New English dioceses were envisaged in the 1911 bull, and in 1917 Brentwood was set up with Bernard Ward, the great ecclesiastical historian, as its first Bishop. Bourne's plan for a diocese of Cambridge, in the same year, did not mature, but in 1924 the diocese of Lancaster was separated from Liverpool. Bourne also unsuccessfully sought the reunification of London by a merging of the dioceses of Southwark and Westminster. After the rearrangements, England and Wales comprised twenty-two sees. The numbers of Catholics continued to increase. Indeed, it was a noted feature of English Catholicism in the years between the two world wars that its expansion continued at a time when the Protestant churches were in numerical decline. The rate of increase, however, was less than it should have been to keep pace with natural population advances. There were some 1,710,000 Catholics in 1912; 2,360,000 in 1939; 2,837,000 in 1951; and about 5,600,000 in 1962. The apparent jump in the later estimate indicates, not a sudden mass conversion, but different statistical techniques: early figures are based upon the returns in the annual *Catholic*

Directory; later ones on the more realistic assessments of the Newman Demographic Society. Figures for priests are more easily known: there were 3,800 in 1914; 5,600 in 1939; and 6,643 in 1950, after which time a slow decline began to set in. Contemporaries often emphasized the contribution made by conversion to the Catholic growth, but though this doubtless added to the morale of the institution and to the professional-class element, it was not statistically very significant. There were 9,000 conversions in 1917; 12,075 in 1929; 8,319 in 1943, and 11,520 in 1948. Distribution of Catholics followed the pattern evident in the nineteenth century: the Church was strongest in the north—in Durham, the North Riding of Yorkshire, Cumberland and Northumberland—in Lancashire and Cheshire, in Warwickshire, and in London. Growth in the south-east of the country was the only real change from the pattern of the preceding century. A large number of Catholics lived in Middlesex as well as in London proper by the mid-twentieth century. The Church was, as in the immediate past, largely urban therefore. Only in Lancashire and Durham was there an established rural Catholic population. It was also, still, of largely working-class composition in the parishes: a continuing contrast with the Established Church.

The national leaders of Catholicism in the first half of the twentieth century were also of humbler social origin than the leaders of the Church of England. Bourne, Hinsley, and Griffin were not working class: they came from lower-middle-class backgrounds and were reared in an atmosphere of Roman ecclesiasticism which made them, somehow, virtually classless in English terms. They were, as already noticed, administrators rather than scholars, men of efficiency, duty, and devotion, rather than figures of interestingly rich resonance as their Victorian predecessors had tended to be. Their achievement in sustaining and expanding the sheer physical capacity of the Church—the schools especially—was extraordinarily impressive; their sensitivity to the opinions of the laity and the lower clergy perhaps rather less so. The impression is of a Church which had become confident and routinized: splendid in its pastoral machinery, but in some sense lacking the genius of inventiveness.

Cardinal Bourne succeeded Vaughan at Westminster in 1903. Evelyn Waugh's hard judgement—that he was 'singularly disqualified from normal social intercourse'—does him enormous injustice, but he was certainly a man of unobtrusive style. Francis Bourne's father was a civil servant, his mother was Irish. He was born in Clapham in 1861, and educated at Ushaw and St Edmund's College, Ware. His subsequent preparation for the ministry was at the Hammersmith seminary (St Thomas) from 1880, at St Sulpice in Paris, from 1881—which left a particularly marked legacy of discipline and austerity—and at Louvain from 1883. He was ordained priest in 1885 and served a number of curacies in the diocese of Southwark. In 1889 he founded Wonersh, the diocesan seminary, with some forty pupils. He was raised to episcopal rank as coadjutor to Dr Butt of Southwark in 1895, and succeeded to the diocese in 1897. In 1903 Propaganda appointed him to act as Superior of chaplains in the British Army; the British Government approved the appointment. Then, in 1903, he was unexpectedly named by Rome to succeed Vaughan: he was the youngest of the English bishops, and a reign at Westminster of thirty-two years followed. He was made a cardinal in 1911. Bourne's general outlook was quite closely related to that of his contemporaries in English public life. He exposed no eccentricities; he was neither especially conservative nor especially progressive. He was responsive to events and absorbed the consensus of most cautious men. In a pastoral of 1899, for example, he endorsed the Boer War, and in 1914 he gave articulate support to the allied war aims, visited the troops on the front in France, and defended Benedict XV against the charge of being sympathetic to Germany. By the 1930s, along with other observers, he lamented the European upheavals as symptoms of large changes: 'the drifting of civilization from all moorings'. His social attitudes were enlightened. In 1919, as he surveyed the prospects for post-war reconstruction, he pointed to 'the menace of class warfare', and spoke out against social injustices. There was a need, he said, for considerable social and economic adjustment to secure better working conditions and remuneration for the working classes. Yet in 1926 he preached against the General Strike, denying it any moral basis, as 'a direct challenge to a lawfully constituted authority'—the State—and 'therefore a sin against the obedience which we owe to God'. He was not, however, an opponent of strike action as such, and became in these years a vehement opponent of uncontrolled capitalism. He was also opposed to undue growth of the State, fearing the consequences for the priority of the family, the very centre of Catholic understanding of the social order. In some minor things he had prophetic vision, as in a speech of 1925 in favour of a Channel Tunnel. In ecclesiastical matters his prophetic capacity was more austerely exercised; he was an *apparat* man and not a reformer. Most existing accounts of his work at Westminster, however, undervalue the extent of his concern for the welfare of his clergy and the depth of his own devotional life. He was enthusiastic in his support of a wide range of organizations, from the Catholic Social Guild to the Boy Scouts (there was a 'Cardinal's Own' troop of the latter at Westminster). His biographer, Ernest Oldmeadow, editor of the *Tablet* from 1923, referred to reservations about Bourne which 'sometimes degenerated from legitimate criticism to unworthy intrigue'. But the Church under his guidance was more at peace internally than at any time in the preceding century. Mgr. Ronald Knox disclosed more of himself than of Bourne when he observed: 'I never failed, in his presence, to feel like a fag taking a note round to some tremendous blood at school.' Knox's school was Eton, Bourne's was Ushaw. There was a difference.

Illness began to enfold Bourne from 1932, and in the early hours of the first day of 1935 he died. His heart was placed in the chapel at Wonersh and his body was deposited at St Edmund's, Ware. His successor, Arthur Hinsley, had two obvious similarities. He also was not a scholar, and his appointment to Westminster was, like Bourne's, regarded as controversial. At the time of his elevation he was seventy years old, had lived abroad for most of his professional life, and knew none of the clergy of Westminster. He was promoted because of his administrative capabilities, just as Bourne had been. But his personality was quite different. Whereas Bourne was detached in relationships, Hinsley craved company; where one was formal the other ignored conventions. Hinsley was a thorough Yorkshireman, and spoke with the accent of the north all his life, just like Ullathorne in the nineteenth century. He was born in 1865 and educated at the local village school at Carlton; his mother was Irish and his father a native Yorkshireman. After Ushaw he proceeded to the English College in Rome. There were twelve years in the diocese of Southwark following a dispute with Bishop Gordon of Leeds, and he then returned to Rome, in 1917, as Rector of the *Venerabile*. In 1930, when he was already sixty-three years old, Pius XI appointed him Apostolic Delegate in Africa, and he began a whole new phase of his life in Mombasa. He had never been to Africa: now he was charged with bringing some sort of system into Catholic education in the missions. It was his effectiveness in this work, and his successful relations with the British Colonial Office, which doubtless explained his completely unexpected appointment to Westminster in 1935. Once again, and long after the years at which most men would have attempted it—and in response to his obligation of obedience to the Holy See—he began a new type of work. He seemed to most of the English clergy, as Heenan later put it, like 'a retired and ailing missionary'. They were all to be in for a considerable surprise. For Hinsley's leadership of the English Church was no 'caretaker' interlude. It might, indeed, have been so, for his career at Westminster began to show close similarities to predecessors' in its absorption by administrative detail. But then came the war, and Hinsley's robust faith and social informality—the latter a characteristic which commends itself to the English—were found to be of great service in promoting the war aims and in encouraging national morale. Through broadcasts for the BBC and in visiting the servicemen, and especially the Navy, he became a national figure—a Catholic counterpart to the Anglican Archbishop of Canterbury, William Temple. Both men, in fact, had a comparable outlook on social questions. 'Not since Manning', according to the *Daily Herald*, 'has Britain had a Cardinal who so closely identified himself with the lives of the common people.' He was deeply immersed in the social teachings of the papal encyclicals and combined the resulting emphasis on social reform with opposition to fascism (some of whose positive qualities in Italy he acknowledged) and to the Nazis (whose beliefs he condemned absolutely). 'The creed of Nazism', he wrote to *The Times* in 1940, 'must be denounced as the arch-enemy of mankind.' The Nazis, in turn, condemned him, first as 'a Bolshevik', and then, after his 1943 message in support of the World Jewish Congress, as a 'lover of Jews'. Hinsley attributed the condition of the world in his day to the consequences of secularization: 'it furnishes', he declared in 1941, 'the best plea for Christianity, the most convincing refutation of the materialism and cult of utility on which the advancement of mankind was supposed to depend'. He promoted the aims of the war in 1939 for religious reasons: 'I am convinced that Britain is engaged in this war in the main for the defence of the things of the spirit.' Its purpose was 'the defence of personal and corporate liberty'. It was an engagement with the evils of material ism. In 1940 he said he regarded the war as 'a great conflict between light and darkness', for 'the Christian tradition is being challenged by a new pagan philosophy'. The threat of totalitarianism was an attack on 'the dignity of the individual, the sanctity of the family'. Like Temple, Hinsley died while the war continued, in 1943. Given heroin to lessen his suffering, the great man passed from the world with his rosary in his hand. He had been created a cardinal in 1937.

The Auxiliary Bishop of Birmingham, Bernard Griffin, succeeded as Archbishop of Westminster. He had been a student under Hinsley at the *Venerabile* and had already, in Birmingham since 1938, established a reputation for sound judgement and social concern— seen in his co-ordination of Catholic social services in the province. He died in 1956 and was followed by William Godfrey, the Archbishop of Liverpool. He had been Rector of the *Venerabile* from 1930 and had diplomatic experience as first Apostolic Delegate to Britain in 1938. Though not succeeding to the leadership of the English Catholic Church until 1963, the figure of John Heenan was, however, already influential during the reigns of Cardinals Griffin and Godfrey. He had, in fact, been an adviser on public issues to both Hinsley and Griffin. Born in Ilford in 1905, and educated at the Catholic grammar school of Stamford Hill, at Ushaw, and at the *Venerabile*, Heenan was ordained priest in 1930. His father, a civil servant working in the Patent Office, and his mother, came from Ireland. After a curacy in Barking Heenan became parish priest of Manor Park in 1937. There were persistent differences with Dr Doubleday, the Bishop of Brentwood, and in 1947 he became Superior of the Catholic Missionary Society. This body, almost defunct when Heenan was appointed, was concerned with evangelism inside England. He helped to inspire a number of city missions and a general mission which ended in 1950. In the following year he was consecrated as Bishop of Leeds, and moved in 1957 to Liverpool as Archbishop. Heenan was an adaptable conservative, with a wide range of experience: he had travelled extensively, had been an effective wartime broadcaster, an efficient administrator, and—an important quality in the post-war years—a man well able to establish good relations with non-Catholic Christians and secular civic bodies. It was Heenan who was to lead the English Catholics into their first ecumenical encounters.

The Church over which these national leaders presided was still conscious of its modern revival; it continued to be characterized by triumphalism and a strong sense of Catholic identity. A number of great occasions witnessed to this: the Eucharistic Congress in 1908, the consecration of Westminster Cathedral in 1910, the beatification of the English martyrs in 1929, the restoration of the shrine of Our Lady of Walsingham in 1934, the building of Liverpool Cathedral. The last work was not completed until 1967; the original design by Lutyens had been abandoned, and the eventual structure, of Sir Frederick Gibberd, rose upon an enormous crypt begun in the 1930s. At the parish level, the first half of the twentieth century saw some significant shifts in the basis of English Catholicism. Though still largely urban and almost wholly working class, English Catholics were beginning to move into the suburbs, especially in the years between the wars, and were starting to infiltrate the middle classes. The typical unit was still the small urban parish, with church and schools, the multiplication of institutions more or less keeping pace with population increase. In many areas, as in Liverpool and London, the inner-city parishes were still composed predominantly of the Irish or the descendants of earlier Irish immigrants. Irish self-consciousness began to lessen towards the mid-century: witness the decline of St Patrick's Day celebrations amongst Catholics in England and of Irish organizations like the Ancient Order of Hibernians. The partial settlement of the Irish national question in the 1921 Treaty removed a political issue which had fostered Irish self-consciousness within the immigrant population. One of the most remarkable features of these decades was the continued ability of a relatively poor social section to finance the expansion of Catholic facilities. Here the administrative skills of the leadership were used to great advantage. Indeed, for many priests it must have seemed as though fund-raising was their major preoccupation. 'It was money which made the greatest impact on me in my early years as a parish priest', Heenan recalled in his autobiography (entitled *Not the Whole Truth*). In Dr Ward's survey of the Liverpool parish in the later 1950s he found that 95 per cent of Catholics questioned said they contributed to parochial finances. Yet only 1 per cent put financial administration as the first duty of a priest: 50 per cent mentioned the sacraments in this regard, and 64 per cent replied that visiting the parishioners in their houses was the main duty of a priest. Furthermore, as it also turned out, 84 per cent of those questioned actually had been visited at home in the preceding six-week period. When this sort of comprehensive ministry is compared with Anglican parochial work in the same period it will be appreciated that the Catholic effort was both more disciplined and better supported by the sympathy of the people. But it was, before the Second Vatican Council had begun to effect changes, heavily clerical. It was the priest and his curates who ran the men's clubs, the youth club, the schools, the various women's organizations, and so forth.

The exclusivity of Catholic self-identification also fostered social separation. Up until the 1940s the Catholics constituted a distinct sub-culture, but it began to disintegrate rapidly in the post-war years. The extension of secondary education following the 1944 Education Act helped this, especially as Catholic secondary schools drew their pupils from several parishes and so tended to weaken the parish as an inclusive unit. Wartime evacuation of civilian populations affected just the sort of inner-city areas where Catholicism was located, and this, too, weakened traditional social relationships. So did mixed marriages. By the 1940s something like half the Catholics were entering into marriages with non-Catholics and the numbers have continued to rise ever since. The priority given to the schools question by the hierarchy tended to perpetuate a sense of Catholic segregation from general society. It also helped to convert a lot of Catholic public concern into 'pressure-group' activity—just as issues of morality tended to do in the years after the Council. National Catholic organizations have also tended to segregation: the Association of Catholic Trades Unionists, which developed during the Second World War, and the Young Christian Workers' Movement; the Knights of St Columba and the Catenians for the professional-class Catholics; the Catholic Teachers' Federation and the Guild of Saints Luke, Cosmas and Damian for medical doctors; the organization of students in 1942 into the Union of Catholic Students and of graduates (and later of non-graduates) into the Newman Association; the Society of St Vincent de Paul and the Catholic Child Welfare Council of 1929 for charitable and social enterprises; and the Catholic Social Guild for the propagation of Catholic views on social and economic questions. There has also been a vigorous independent Catholic press: the *Catholic Herald*, the *Catholic Times*, the *Universe*; and the periodicals the *Tablet*, the *Month*, *Blackfriars*, the *Dublin*

Review, the *Clergy Review*. Through these various means, and above all through separate education, English Catholicism in the first half of the twentieth century preserved a very distinct sense of its own teachings and its membership of a universal society.

The social and political outlook of the Church, though formally dependent upon the papal encyclicals, had strong local qualities. When Cardinal Vincenzo Vannutelli arrived in London as Legate for the Eucharistic Congress of 1908 he spoke approvingly of 'this land of liberty, freedom and toleration'. These were not political features which had commended themselves to the Church of the *Syllabus of Errors* back in 1864, but by the start of the twentieth century English Catholics, especially, were more conscious than ever of their integration with native political virtues. At the leadership level, the Church spoke of the evils both of uncontrolled capitalism and individualism, and of communism and materialism, in a way which was made to depend upon the social reformist spirit of Leo XIII's *Rerum Novarum* (1891) and Pius XI's *Quadragesimo Anno* (1931). English Catholic leaders also derived their social critique from a domestic tradition which they shared with sections of the Protestant intelligentsia, and which was also to be found well established within the leadership of the Church of England. To look back to the medieval past for an example of just economic principles and social harmony, and to associate Protestantism with the emergence of capitalism, was the hallmark of such Anglican thinkers of the start of the century as William Cunningham, Neville Figgis, and R. H. Tawney. The social criticism of existing society which derived from their vision was subsequently popularized by William Temple, and in the Catholic Church by Hinsley. Cardinal Bourne, also, had interpreted the papal encyclicals in the light of this tradition of thought. In his 1918 pastoral, on the need for post-war social reconstruction, he condemned 'fierce individualism' and remarked that 'the working classes are now in undisguised revolt' for legitimate reasons—because 'England came under the dominion of a capitalistic and oligarchic regime which would have been unthinkable had Catholic ideals prevailed'. Capitalism, he argued, began with Protestantism; since then 'the effect of competition uncontrolled by morals has been to segregate more and more the capitalist from the wage-earning classes'. It was now a Catholic duty to declare 'that persons are of more value than property'—he cited Leo XIII as authority—and he declared that modern criticisms of *laissez-faire* practice had 'points of contact' with Catholic teaching. In fact, they had even more than he acknowledged. But the political application of his social ideals raised difficulties for Bourne: he distinguished between the Labour Party and Labour politics, whose social reformism was to be desired—as he declared at a Catholic rally in 1925—and 'Socialism', which he condemned as unjust. Socialism, in its 'technical sense', he elaborated, attacked legitimate rights of property and brought 'state action into a sphere not within its competence'. Thus he was sceptical of modern collectivism whilst applauding some of the social ameliorations which it achieved. That was to be the conclusion of most English Catholic thought on social and political questions in the first half of the twentieth century. In the same speech of 1925 Bourne also denounced class warfare and promoted the ideal of class co-operation—there were, again, close affinities here with contemporaneous Anglican thinking. He also urged an end to unemployment. Cardinal Hinsley's attitudes were a development of these, moulded by the unfolding of events in Europe in the 1930s. In 1936 the Catholic hierarchy issued a joint pastoral letter on the need to combat the social evils of the time. In his New Year message for 1937, Hinsley called for an end to 'class-hatred provoked by the capitalist system', and said that against both capitalism and communism 'the gospel of love must be opposed to the gospel of greed and hate'. A great rally which he organized at the Albert Hall in September 1937 on 'The Catholic Church and the Social Question', whilst assailing atheistic communism, advanced social reform ideas. 'No state can claim to be constructed rationally or morally', he declared on that occasion, 'when one section of the community has to be heavily taxed to provide for another, at the cost of its natural dignity and independence.' He also condemned those given to a 'parasitic existence', and counselled class harmony to achieve 'a higher good'.

The most active agency for Catholic social progressivism was the Catholic Social Guild, founded in 1909 and supported by both Bourne and Hinsley. It was intended as an educative and propagandist body, to prepare Catholics for social action according to the teachings of the Church: it almost exactly paralleled, in both teaching and policies, the social unions and guilds to be found in the Protestant churches. Local branches soon appeared and by 1939 the

Guild had nearly four thousand members. A Catholic Workers' College was founded in Oxford. There was a considerable output of literature, and a journal, *The Christian Democrat*, started publication in 1921. The Guild came to an end in 1967: it had survived far longer than most of its Protestant counterparts. There had been other associations for Catholic social action, like the Salford Diocesan Federation of 1906, which prepared Catholics for political participation while declining any declared party preference of its own. Bourne had also given Catholic support to the National Council for Social Service. The 'Sword of the Spirit', inaugurated by Hinsley in 1940, and intended to secure 'a return to the principles of international order and Christian freedom' once the totalitarian threat had been overcome, also had a progressive social atmosphere. Hinsley appointed Christopher Dawson, the historian and writer—a convert of 1914—as lay leader of the campaign. But it failed to achieve support with large numbers of ordinary Catholics, perhaps because its internationalism lacked common points of reference.

The emergence of the Welfare State raised some initial problems for the English Catholic leadership. Hinsley's attitude was characteristic: while he welcomed the Beveridge Report as suggesting a new social order which was preferable, as he understood it, to past injustices, he lamented the heightening of State power and the tightening of collectivism which the required reforms introduced. Aspects of the new social planning were certainly thought to be incompatible with Catholic teaching on the priority of the family. The threat corresponded to the diminution of parental rights, as Catholics saw it, in the State school system, and gave an additional incentive to the campaign for denominational schools. Similar fears later led to the withdrawal of Catholic voluntary hospitals from the National Health Service, after Bevan had been unable to accommodate Catholic requests for greater internal autonomy. The Catholic Social Guild, under the secretaryship of Fr. Paul Crane in the 1950s declared some theoretical objections to the Welfare State on the basis of its aggrandizement of government. Yet the general balance of judgement within the Church was to accept the new order of things. That was not, however, so obvious a development as appears from hindsight: in Ireland the Catholic bishops successfully opposed the introduction of a Welfare State in the 1940s and 1950s precisely because of its undermining of family rights.

English Catholic leaders have, in the twentieth century, continued the tradition of avoiding partisan political pronouncements. 'The Catholic Church has no alliance with any political party—she stands outside them all', Bourne declared in a pastoral of 1904. His view of Christian political involvement was actually that of Temple also: that the Church should define general principles but leave particular applications to the initiative of the laity. In 1925 he told an East End gathering in London that the obligation of the Church was 'to lay down the moral law', and added, 'she has never claimed, and has never exercised, any right to deal directly with what we call political parties'. At the present time, he was able to conclude, no political party in England was incompatible with Catholicism. The Church was nevertheless drawn into political issues. The Irish question, at the start of the century, persisted in attracting the concern of the Irish masses of the industrial parishes. The English Catholic leaders, who were nearly all Home Rulers in personal sympathy, avoided partisan declarations. Occasionally particular events in the super-charged atmosphere at the end of the Great War revealed common Catholic feelings: as at the beatification of Oliver Plunket in 1920, or the solemn requiem for Terence MacSwiney in Southwark Cathedral in the same year. Bourne refused to receive the Australian Archbishop Mannix, banned by the British Government from visiting Ireland, in order to avoid controversy. The Irish settlement of 1921–2 removed the problem, at least temporarily.

It is interesting to notice that the appeal of the corporate state and of fascism, felt so strongly among sections of the Irish Church in the 1930s, was not greatly echoed among English Catholics—and certainly not among Catholic working-class people. A minority of the English Catholic intelligentsia, and a few priests, had some admiration for Mussolini's reconstruction of Italy, and the Spanish Civil War elicited sympathy for the plight of the Catholics in areas controlled by the communists and anarchists. In 1937 Ronald Knox preached a sermon in support of Franco. But Eric Gill's warnings, in letters to the *Catholic Herald*, about the dangers of the English Church aligning itself with fascism, exaggerated the possibility of this ever happening. English Catholicism was too English in its social and political outlook. Whatever its adhesion to formal ideological declarations, like the papal encyclicals, its actual practices were inevitably derived from a thoroughly English empiricism. Even 'distributism,' which had a vogue among the Catholic literary and artistic élite in the 1930s, was a characteristically 'arts-and-crafts' vision rather than an expression of a genuinely systematic political ideology. Its roots lay in opposition to collectivism—in Hilaire Belloc's *The Servile State* (1913), in G. K. Chesterton's rejection of what he called 'the twin evils of Capitalism and Communism', in Eric Gill's lusty medieval artisans with their folk-weaves and rustic liberty, and in Fr. Vincent McNabb's 'back-to-the-land' alternative to industrial society. There were, again, numerous Anglican and secular counterparts in the years between the wars. The Distributive League projected a land of small freeholders, monetary reform and self-sufficiency, with no political parties. It looked like nothing so much as the old Chartist Land Plan of the 1840s. Because it envisaged the end of politics, distributism can hardly be categorized as an exception to the general Catholic avoidance of political involvement.

Most Catholic parishioners supported the popular parties—the Liberals at the start of the century, and then the Labour Party: it was an inheritance of the Irish immigration. Systematic socialism had little appeal, and the formation in Leeds of a Catholic Socialist Society in 1906 was not emulated. But the Church did encourage Catholics to participate in labour organization, as a necessary application of Catholic teachings on social justice. The National Conference of Catholic Trades Unionists tried unsuccessfully to prevent the Labour Party from a formal adhesion to socialist principles (which it declared in 1918). There was a further complication in 1942, when the TUC resolved in favour of the abolition of all denominational schools. Yet Catholics have taken a leading part in trade-union developments in the present century, and have fully implemented the teaching of the leadership about lay application to the details of general Christian principles. The nearest the Church collectively has come to political action was over the education question, with the formation in 1945 of the Catholic Parents and Electors Association. This body, with numerous local branches, was a natural evolution out of existing diocesan associations. It carried Catholic opposition to the terms of the 1944 Education Act into the general election of 1950. Candidates' records were scrutinized, and they were questioned publicly about their attitude to denominational schools.

The education question, indeed, was the major concern of the bishops and clergy in the first half of the twentieth century. In Britain, Heenan said in an interview for *Osservatore Romano* at the start of the Vatican Council in 1962, 'our greatest preoccupation is school building'. The preservation of the faith and morals of children, and the education of parents into a sense of responsibility, which separate schools achieved, was regarded as the great strength of English Catholicism—as the sure foundation established by the nineteenth-century Church. Cardinal Bourne's first pastoral, like Manning's half a century before, was taken up with educational questions. The problem facing the Church was twofold: how to finance the building and maintenance of schools in view of the relative poverty of most working-class Catholic parishes; how to persuade the governments of the day that Catholic tax-payers were entitled to full and equal State grants for their own denominational schools alongside the national system of education. In a famous declaration of 1929, the hierarchy acknowledged the right of the State 'to see that citizens receive due education sufficient to enable them to discharge the duties of citizenship'. But in doing so, 'the State must not interfere with parental responsibility, nor hamper the reasonable liberty of parents in their choice of a school for their children'. The issue thus involved fundamental Catholic natural-law teachings about the priority of the family over the State. Differences were also sharpened by the increasingly divergent attitude of the State to such moral issues as marriage legislation. The passage of the Deceased Wife's Sister Act in 1907, and the extension of the legal grounds of divorce in 1937, had suggested to Catholic leaders that the English State could no longer be regarded as the guarantor of traditional Christian morality: it was therefore dangerous to entrust the moral education of children to agencies of the State. Similar problems were being encountered by the Catholic hierarchy in the United States at the same time, and they were, of course, long familiar in Europe. Pius XI's encyclical *Casti Connubii* in 1930, on birth-control, also heightened the sense of difference between Catholic and secular concepts of moral responsibility. The schools issue was not, therefore, a matter of doctrinal or catechistical exactitude only: it involved the whole concept of the preservation of Catholic spiritual culture and a belief in the inseparability of sacred and secular learning in the classroom. 'The disastrous results of excluding Christianity from the education of youth are plain to all who have eyes to see', Hinsley observed in 1942: totalitarianism in Europe, he contended, was a fruit of the new 'paganism'.

By the time of the Education Act of 1944, there were 1,260 Catholic elementary (primary) schools, with 400,000 children, and an increasing number of secondary schools. In the typical small, urban Catholic parishes of the large industrial areas, something like 90 per cent of Catholic children received denominational education. It was a very considerable achievement, but the financial strain in keeping the system going, and expanding it, and the almost permanent need to protect the government subsidies from political opposition, occupied a great amount of the leaders' time. The assault by the Free Churches and the Liberal Party upon the Balfour Act of 1902 was unrelenting; before 1914 some twenty legislative attempts were made to end the 'dual system' of education. After the Liberals' success in the 1906 general election, Bourne went to some lengths to make it clear that however much the Catholic Church would oppose Liberal educational policies there was 'no quarrel with any particular party'. Augustine Birrell's Education Bill of 1906 was intended to conciliate Free Churchmen and secularists. The 'dual system' was to be abandoned, and all schools in receipt of public financial aid were to come fully under local government control. The Anglicans joined the Catholics in opposition to the proposals. A joint pastoral of the Catholic hierarchy appealed to the House of Lords for justice. After lengthy differences between the two Houses, the Bill was withdrawn. Subsequent similar attempts were also unsuccessful. The political result was a practical, if reluctant, dependence of the Catholic leadership upon the Conservative Party. An Act of 1936 empowered local authorities to pay 75 per cent of the cost of new schools and of improvements to existing ones. But it was the high-water mark of public assistance to denominational education in England. By that time the Anglicans were surrendering a number of their schools to the local authorities, and accepting the 'agreed syllabus' arrangements for religious education which had spread since 1924: the acceptance, that is to say, of non-denominational and 'unsectarian' Christian formulae. In the debate over the Education Bill of 1944, also, the Anglicans tended to accept the offered terms as realistic, whereas the Catholics rejected them. The Butler Act perpetuated the 'dual system' but divided the denominational schools into two categories. 'Controlled' schools were to be fully maintained by public finance, but were to lose exclusive Church management and were to teach only 'agreed syllabuses'. The 'voluntary aided' schools retained their religious autonomy but were to secure only 50 per cent maintenance grants. It was a blow to the Catholic Church. 'We have not received justice', Archbishop Griffin, who had succeeded Hinsley after an interregnum at Westminster, concluded: the Catholic Church declined 'controlled' status for its schools. The *Tablet* observed that Parliament was accepting 'the idea of a non-institutional Christianity'. The hierarchy declared that it could 'never accept' the legislation, and launched a campaign to finance the continuation and extension of its own system. In 1949 they estimated that the cost would be up to £60 million—to be, as they lamented, 'sweated out of the working men'. It was, nevertheless, one of the most impressive of Catholic achievements: that the parents' associations established to co-ordinate the campaign, and the parish priests in the localities, were successful in extending Catholic education in the years after the war. Through representations to governments of the day the State grant was progressively increased, first to 60 per cent and then up to 85 per cent.

Catholic intellectual life in the first half of the twentieth century was in some respects affected by the condemnation of modernism. In 1893, in the encyclical *Providentissimus Deus*, Leo XIII had set limits to free biblical criticism, and in 1907 St Pius X's decree *Lamentabili Sane* listed sixty-five errors of the modernists. In a second encyclical of the same year, *Pascendi Dominici Gregis*, scholastic theology was upheld as the authentic model for learning in the Church. The purpose of the encyclicals, and of the English hierarchy who looked to them for guidance, was not to discourage intellectual enquiry or the pursuit of knowledge for its own sake: their object was to see that Catholic scholarship was conducted within the consensus of the faithful, that academic undertakings should be within the *magisterium* of the Church. The case against George Tyrrell was precisely that he developed ideas without particular reference to the teaching office of the Church. Tyrrell's writings have enjoyed a new popularity with Catholic intellectual opinion in recent years: he has now seemed to be a prophet of contemporary questionings of authority. His first unorthodoxies appeared in 1899, with an article on Catholic doctrine entitled 'A Perverted Devotion'. In the ensuing controversy, Tyrrell got the support of von Hügel. In 1903 he circulated a dismissive essay on the pastoral letter of the bishops on 'Liberal Catholicism'. Then came a number of works in which his opposition to received Catholic notions was very evident. In 1907 he wrote to *The Times* to protest about the encyclicals of St Pius X, and in 1908 he published *Medievalism*, a bitter criticism of the Church. He was excommunicated in 1907 and when he died, in 1909, he was refused Catholic burial. Yet despite this unhappy episode, the bishops were anxious to avoid taking disciplinary action over independent scholarship, and Cardinal Bourne refused to bow to requests to silence Wilfrid Ward, editor of the *Dublin Review* between 1906 and 1916, when he used the journal to defend modernism. Biblical criticism was too easily identified with Protestantism, too. It was an additional impediment to Catholic acceptance of it. 'I grew up in a world in which Protestants, who had just proved that Rome did not believe the Bible, were excitedly discovering that they did not believe the Bible themselves', Chesterton wrote in 1926. Subsequent encyclicals from Rome softened some of the hostility to contemporary intellectual culture: thus the effect of Pius XII's *Divino Afflati Spiritu* in 1943. But *Humani Generis* in 1950 repeated some of the former censures in revised language. The result of this tradition was undoubtedly inhibiting for Catholic scholarship in England, and the first half of the twentieth century saw a certain paucity of inventive theological writing. There was, however, some distinguished Catholic historical scholarship, especially within the religious orders.

It was a time of great strength for the orders. The Dominicans, under the leadership of Fr. Bede Jarrett, and the Benedictines both expanded in these years. The English Benedictine Congregation established Worth Priory in 1933, and made Ealing Priory independent of Downside in 1947. The great expansion of religious orders of women began to show signs of coming to an end in the 1940s, but the rate before then had been extraordinary—especially of the stricter orders like the Poor Clares, who had nineteen houses by 1950, most of them founded in the preceding two decades. The Benedictines produced a group of important historians: Cardinal Aidan Gasquet, Dom Cuthbert Butler, and Dom David Knowles—the last became Regius Professor at Cambridge. The Jesuits produced Fr. Herbert Thurston, whose influence as a writer in nearly fifty years at Farm

Street was enormous. Archbishop David Mathew and Fr. Philip Hughes added further distinction to Catholic historical scholarship. Catholic contributions to the general literary scene were also very notable, though with the exception of Hilaire Belloc they were nearly all converts: Ronald Knox, G. K. Chesterton, Evelyn Waugh, and Graham Greene. Knox was regarded by Heenan as 'perhaps the greatest figure in the Church of the twentieth century'. The son of an Anglican bishop, he was converted in 1917 and became Catholic Chaplain at Oxford in 1926. His writings included *A Spiritual Aeneid* (1918) and *The Belief of Catholics* (1927); but he was best known for his translation of the Bible—a work begun in 1939 and completed in 1955. He died in 1957. The most influential Catholic architect of the period was Sir Giles Gilbert Scott, designer of the Anglican Cathedral at Liverpool and of the nave at Downside Abbey church. The most important artist was Eric Gill, self-styled 'stone-carver', whose Stations of the Cross in Westminster Cathedral (created between 1914 and 1918) were his least controversial artistic offerings. He had been converted in 1913 and set up a community of Dominican Tertiaries at Ditchling. As an articulate socialist he also became something of a hammer of the Catholic Establishment. He once remarked that St Peter's in Rome looked 'exactly like the Ritz Palace Hotel'. The Catholic presence in the universities achieved less colourful and more respected attention in the first half of the century. In Oxford, Fr. Martin d'Arcy made Campion Hall a centre of intellectual life; in Cambridge the chaplaincy of Mgr. Alfred Gilbey had a considerable spiritual influence within the university generally and procured a number of noted conversions.

The Catholic Church, indeed, was by the middle of the twentieth century an accepted part of the English religious pluralism. There was, it is true, occasional continuing evidence of the long English tradition of anti-Catholicism, both at the popular level and through the action of evangelical Protestant activists. Asquith was induced to ban a street procession at the Eucharistic Congress of 1908, for example, after fears for public order were canvassed following Protestant threats to intervene and break it up. That was not, furthermore, Bourne's first acquaintance with such difficulties. In 1905 he had led a public procession in honour of Our Lady of Willesden which local Protestants had sought to get banned through an application to the magistrates under the terms of the Catholic

Emancipation Act of 1829. But there was a continuing slow decline of public hostility to Catholicism, especially within the governing circles. Anti-Catholic feeling, in fact, declined at about the same rate as involvement with organized religion in general in society. Legislation in 1926 removed many surviving formal Catholic disabilities from the statute-book: some Protestants objected. They had done so before, in 1910, when the Declaration made by George V at his accession to the throne was modified by the Government to remove offensive references to the Catholic religion. Yet diplomatic links were established between England and Rome. In 1908 St Pius X sent the first Legate to England, for the Eucharistic Congress, in three hundred and fifty years. In 1914 Sir Henry Howard headed a special British mission to the Vatican, and in the following year, under Benedict XV, the British Legation to the Vatican was permanently established. In 1938 William Godfrey was appointed as first Apostolic Delegate in London. A symbol of the new relations came with the death of Cardinal Hinsley in 1943: nearly all the members of the Government attended his funeral, something unthinkable in the preceding century. The experience of servicemen in the two world wars must also have assisted better understanding between Protestants and Catholics. In the First World War, in particular, the Catholic chaplains were greatly admired for their professionalism and their clarity of purpose. By 1918 there were almost six hundred Catholic chaplains in the Army, under a bishop (Mgr. Keatinge) appointed by Rome. The Government, in fact, provided a more favourable ratio of chaplains to men for the Catholics because the soldiers expected a regular sacramental ministry. A contrast with the Anglicans became apparent to many. Guy Chapman, later Professor of History at Leeds, recalled his impressions. 'The Church of Rome sent a man into action mentally and spiritually cleaned,' he observed; 'the Church of England could only offer you a cigarette.' Maurice Child, an Anglican clergyman rejected for chaplaincy service, had replied, in answer to the question 'what would you do for a dying man?' put to him by the Chaplain-General, 'Hear his confession and give him absolution.' The correct answer should have been 'Give him a cigarette and take any last message he may have for his family.' The Catholic priests were also, in general, more accustomed to a ministry among the working classes than the Anglicans, and this meant that they did not suffer the culture-shock which so many Church of England clergy encountered in the trenches. Social mobility was more advanced by the time of the Second World War, and the contrasts were less noticeable. Some eccentric fragments of anti-Catholicism still emerged. In 1942 H. G. Wells wrote an article in the *Sunday Dispatch* encouraging the Catholics to depose Pius XII and the allies to bomb Rome.

The 1920s had seen the revival of the idea of some sort of reunion of the Catholic and Anglican Churches. The leadership of neither Church was directly involved, though the Archbishop of Canterbury, for the Anglicans, was at least kept abreast of developments by the participants; Cardinal Bourne was not. The conversations at Malines, held on four occasions between 1921 and 1926, were the work of the same men whose explorations had, in 1896, ended in the condemnation of Anglican orders by the papacy. Once again neither Lord Halifax for the Anglicans nor the Abbé Portal for the Catholics was supported by any substantial body of opinion in their Churches. This time Cardinal Mercier, the Belgian primate, acted as convenor, with himself, Portal, and Mgr. van Roey on the Catholic side, and Halifax, Walter Frere (Superior of the Community of the Resurrection) and Dr Armitage Robinson (Dean of Wells) on the Anglican. The conversations were only made public in 1923, and it at once became apparent that they rested upon insecure understandings of each other's position by both parties. It was extraordinary that Cardinal Gasquet, a veteran of the 1890s inquiries, was not consulted. Yet both Benedict XV and Pius XI (who succeeded him in 1922) approved of the discussions. In 1923 the teams were strengthened by the addition of two Catholic Church historians, Mgr. Pierre Battifol and Fr. Hippolyte Hemmer, and the Anglican Bishop Gore and Dr Kidd, Warden of Keble College, Oxford. The Anglicans had, as their authority for proceeding, a resolution in favour of Christian unity from the Lambeth Conference of 1920; but the Catholics had only the tacit approval of the papacy acting on the supposition that what was intended was the surrender of the Anglicans to the claims of Rome. Bourne was basically hostile, and the visit to Rome of Ernest Oldmeadow, editor of the *Tablet*, to consult with Cardinal Merry del Val about the previous condemnations of reunion discussions by the Vatican (in 1864 and 1896), may well have been intended to prepare the grounds for a rejection of the whole enterprise. In the event, with Mercier's death in 1926 the discussions came to an end. Canon Moyes, who had also taken part in the 1890s inquiries, remarked: 'Perhaps the best thing that comes of such attempts is the lesson that nothing ever comes of them.' The English Catholic Church was certainly, at the time, unprepared for any *rapprochement* with Protestantism. Pius XI's encyclical of 1928, *Mortalium Animos*, while making no direct reference to Malines, upheld Catholic teachings on the unitary nature of the Church and condemned co-operation with Protestant bodies established according to necessarily false premises. That was the policy of Hinsley: co-operation but not union. It was especially suited to social and international issues, and his 'Sword of the Spirit' movement of 1940 began with a joint statement in *The Times*, signed by the Anglican archbishops and by the Moderator of the Free Churches, in support of Pius XII's Five Peace Points. Slowly, over the ensuing decade, the spirit of co-operation began to extend itself. 'We did not use the word "ecumenical"', Cardinal Heenan later recalled, 'but we were already thinking and talking in terms of Christian Unity.' Developments of Marian dogma, and especially the promulgation in 1950 of the doctrine of the Assumption of the Virgin, introduced some new impediments from the Protestant point of view. But in 1960 an enormous impetus was given by the visit of the Anglican Archbishop Fisher of Canterbury to Pope John XXIII.

Among European Catholics, meanwhile—and especially in the churches of Germany, Belgium, and Holland—there were already, in the later 1950s, new stirrings of theological radicalism, preparing for the upheavals of the next decade. Ecumenism was an integral part of the new spirit. In England, on the eve of the Council called by John XXIII, a Secretariat for Christian Unity was set up by Heenan—who was a member of the Roman Secretariat for Unity—at the Heythrop Conference of 1962. His pastoral letter as Archbishop of Liverpool, in March 1962, with its code of conduct for Catholics involved in discussions with other Christians, achieved a wide acceptance. Heenan's participation was a sign that in England the impulse for Christian unity extended much further into the Church than might have seemed likely: it was not merely the partisan enthusiasm of groups of liberals. The English Catholics were mostly out of touch with the advanced thought of northern Europeans, however, and were soon to be surprised when they encountered their impatience for change at the Council. With some confidence, born of the successful re-establishment of the faith in England after centuries of persecution and civil disadvantage, the Catholic bishops could look to the future for further quiet expansion. And so they set off for Rome, in October 1962, to take up residence at the English College for the duration of the Council. Although they were unaware of it, a distinct phase of English Catholic history was drawing to an end. Through the tradition they had inherited from the most difficult times, English Catholicism was well placed for conservative adaptation—and also for insistence on fundamentals. 'Belief in God', Cardinal Hinsley had once observed, in relation to the need for proper education in Christian principles, 'is the unshakeable foundation of all social order and of all responsibility on earth.'

Suggested further reading

J. Altholz, *The Liberal Catholic Movement in England*, 1962.

W. L. Arnstein, *Protestant versus Catholic in Mid-Victorian England*, 1982.

J. C. H. Aveling, *The Handle and the Axe: The Catholic Recusants in England from Reformation to Emancipation*, 1976.

L. Barmann, *Von Hügel and the Modernist Crisis in England*, 1972.

G. A. Beck (ed.), *The English Catholics, 1850–1950*, 1950.

D. A. Bellenger (ed.) *English and Welsh Priests, 1558–1800*, 1984.

J. Bossy, *The English Catholic Community, 1570–1850*, 1975.

C. Butler, *The Life and Times of Bishop Ullathorne, 1806–1889*, 1926.

W. O. Chadwick, *Newman*, 1983.

P. Coman, *Catholics and the Welfare State*, 1977.

J. Denvir, *The Irish in Britain: From the earliest times to the fall and death of Parnell*, 1892.

C. S. Dessain, *John Henry Newman*, 1966.

E. Duffy (ed.), *Challoner and his Church: A Catholic Bishop in Georgian England*, 1981.

A. Dures, *English Catholicism, 1558–1642*, 1983.

B. Fothergill, *Nicholas Wiseman*, 1963.

A. Gasquet, *Lord Acton and his Circle*, 1906.

D. Gwynn, *The Second Spring, 1818–1852: The Catholic Revival in England*, 1942.

M. J. Havran, *The Catholics in Caroline England*, 1962.

J. C. Heenan, *Cardinal Hinsley*, 1944.

———— *Not the Whole Truth*, 1971; *A Crown of Thorns*, 1974.

B. Hemphill, *The Early Vicars Apostolic of England, 1685–1750*, 1954.

J. Hickey, *Urban Catholics: Urban Catholicism in England and Wales from 1829 to the present day*, 1967.

J. D. Holmes, *More Roman than Rome: English Catholicism in the nineteenth century*, 1978.

M. D. R. Leys, *Catholics in England, 1559–1829: A social history*, 1961.

B. Magee, *The English Recusants: A study of the post-Reformation Catholic survival and the operation of the recusancy laws*, 1938.

B. Martin, *John Henry Newman*, 1982.

D. Mathew, *Catholicism in England: The portrait of a minority*, 1936.

V. A. McClelland, *Cardinal Manning: His public life and influence*, 1962.

A. Morey, *The Catholic Subjects of Elizabeth I*, 1978.

E. R. Norman, *Anti-Catholicism in Victorian England*, 1968.

―――― *The English Catholic Church in the Nineteenth Century*, 1984.

E. Oldmeadow, *Francis Cardinal Bourne*, 1940.

B. and M. Pawley, *Rome and Canterbury through Four Centuries*, 1974.

E. S. Purcell, *The Life of Cardinal Manning*, 1895.

E. E. Reynolds, *The Roman Catholic Church in England and Wales: A short history*, 1973.

―――― *Campion and Parsons: The Jesuit Mission of 1580–1*, 1980.

J. G. Snead-Cox, *The Life of Cardinal Vaughan*, 1910.

M. Trevor, *Newman: Pillar of the Cloud; Light in Winter*, 1962.

B. Ward, *The Eve of Catholic Emancipation*, 1911.

―――― *The Sequel to Catholic Emancipation*, 1915.

C. K. Ward, *Priests and People: A study in the sociology of religion*, 1961.

W. Ward, *The Life and Times of Cardinal Wiseman*, 1897.

―――― *W. G. Ward and the Catholic Revival*, 2nd edn., 1912.

E. I. Watkin, *Roman Catholicism in England: From the Reformation to 1950*, 1957.

H. E. Williams, *The Venerable English College, Rome*, 1979.

Index

Politics, involvement in 63–4, 81–2, 116, 119
Poor Clares, 124
Pope, Alexander, 51
Pope, powers of, 26–7, 29, 38, 86, 90, 100, 103
popes: Benedict XIV, 42; Benedict XV, 110, 126, 127; Clement XIV, 48; Gregory XIII, 18; Gregory XVI, 66, 67; John XXIII, 128; Leo XIII, 82, 90, 92, 94, 101, 105, 116, 123; Paul V, 33; Pius IV, 10; Pius V, 12; Pius VII, 58, 62; Pius IX, 67, 68, 85, 89; Puis X, 70, 123, 126; Pius XI, 116, 121, 127, 128; Pius XII, 124, 128
Popish Plot, 38
Portal, Fernand, 94, 127
Poynter, William, 59, 61, 62, 65
Prayer Book (1552), 10
Press, Catholic, 115–16
Pretender, Old, 41; Young, 25–6, 41
priest holes, 13
priests, mission, 7, 13, 16, 19, 22, 28, 30, 42, 48, 66; harbouring of, 13; expulsion of, 15; secular, 16, 24, 25, 30, 32, 42, 44–5, 49, 66; authority of, 107
Prior Park, 66, 74, 79, 85
Propaganda, Congregation of, 41, 42, 44, 64, 67, 70, 76, 79, 80, 81, 85, 108, 110
Protestant Association, 55
Protestantism, 4, 5, 9, 19, 41, 46, 48, 86, 106, 116, 124; Erastianism of, 7, 26, 72; *see also* Protestants
Protestants 2, 8, 10, 33, 125–6; burnings of, 9; Dissenters, 8, 37, 46, 59; theologians, 86
Pugin, Augustus W., 72, 75–6, 86
Purcell, E. S., 88
Puritans, 8, 37

Quarantotti, Jean B., 62

Rambler, 98, 99, 104
Rebellion of Northern Earls, 12
Rebellion of 1745, 41
recusants, 14, 29; character of, 1; trial of, 13; fines on 34, 36
Redemptorists, 74
Reformation, the, 1, 27
Reunion of Churches, 94, 127–8
Ridley, Nicholas, 9
Ridolfi Plot, 12

Rock, Daniel, 67
Rome, English College at, 17–18, 21, 25, 42, 64, 83, 129
Rosminians, 74
Rossetti, Carlo, 35
Rump Parliament, 36
Rural Deans, 45
Russell, Lord John, 68

St Bartholomew's Day, Massacre of, 12
St Edmund's College, 53, 59, 79, 84, 85, 93, 101
St Germain, 40
St Joseph's Missionary Society, 93
St Omer, 21
St Winifrid, Holy Well of, 26
Sales, Francis de, 52, 53
Salesians, 74
Salford, 95, 118
Sander, Nicholas, 18
Savile, Sir George, 55
schools, denominational, 76–7, 78, 96, 109, 118, 120, 121–3; numbers of, 122
Scotland, 55
Sedgley Park, 53, 79
Sergeant, John, 44–5
Sheldon, William, 55
Simpson, Richard, 104
Smith, James, 45
Smith, Richard, 43
Southwell, Robert, 12, 21
Southworth, John, 36
Spencer, George, 72
Stafford, Viscount, 39
Stockport, 71
Stone, 74, 75
Stonor, John, 41, 54
Stonyhurst, 78–9
Stourton, Lord, 14, 27
Strickland, Thomas, 41
Stuarts, 8, 33; Catholic support of, 36, 41; restoration of, 37
Stukeley, Thomas, 18
Sunderland, Earl of, 39
Supremacy, Royal, 9, 10; Oath of, 10, 13, 15, 21, 59, 60, 62
Surrey, Earl of, 64
Syllabus of Errors, 90, 91, 102, 103, 116

Tablet, The, 81, 93, 111, 115, 123, 127
Talbot, Mgr. George, 89
Talbot, James, 53